201 TIPS TO START AND BUILD YOUR OWN BUSINESS

Jay Miletsky

Course Technology PTR
A part of Cengage Learning

COURSE TECHNOLOGY
CENGAGE Learning™

Australia, Brazil, Japan, Korea, Mexico, Singapore, Spain, United Kingdom, United States

COURSE TECHNOLOGY
CENGAGE Learning™

201 Tips to Start and Build Your Own Business
Jay Miletsky

Publisher and General Manager, Course Technology PTR:
Stacy L. Hiquet

Associate Director of Marketing:
Sarah Panella

Manager of Editorial Services:
Heather Talbot

Marketing Manager:
Mark Hughes

Acquisitions Editor:
Mitzi Koontz

Project Editor:
Kate Shoup

Copy Editor:
Kate Shoup

Interior Layout:
Jill Flores

Cover Designer:
Mike Tanamachi

Indexer:
Kelly Talbot

Proofreader:
Sandi Wilson

Course Technology, a part of Cengage Learning
20 Channel Center Street
Boston, MA 02210
USA

For product information and technology assistance, contact us at **Cengage Learning Customer & Sales Support 1-800-354-9706**

For permission to use material from this text or product, submit all requests online at **cengage.com/permissions** Further permissions questions can be emailed to **permissionrequest@cengage.com**

All trademarks are the property of their respective owners.

Library of Congress Control Number: 2009941737

ISBN-13: 978-1-4354-5548-1

ISBN-10: 1-4354-5548-7

Cengage Learning is a leading provider of customized learning solutions with office locations around the globe, including Singapore, the United Kingdom, Australia, Mexico, Brazil, and Japan. Locate your local office at: **international.cengage.com/region**

Cengage Learning products are represented in Canada by Nelson Education, Ltd.

For your lifelong learning solutions, visit **courseptr.com**.

Visit our corporate website at **cengage.com**

Printed in Canada
1 2 3 4 5 6 7 11 10 09

This book is dedicated to everybody who played an important part of my early career as an entrepreneur. This long list includes clients who gave me a shot when I didn't deserve one such as Henry Vander Plaat, Brian Phelan, Frank Simons, Steve Klein, Barry Brandman, and Michael Hand; my business partner, Deirdre Breakenridge; and of course my parents.

ACKNOWLEDGMENTS

Thanks to everybody at Cengage Learning. You guys continue to rock! Big thanks to Kate Shoup—your politics might be out of whack, but you're a hell of an editor! Thanks go to my family, Cindi, Chris, and Jackie. And a special thanks to everybody who has ever believed in me as well as everybody who has ever doubted me—you all pushed me to do better!

ABOUT THE AUTHOR

Jay Miletsky is CEO and executive creative director of Mango (formerly PFS Marketwyse), a leading marketing communications agency in the New York metro area. His marketing work has included successful consultation and campaigns for companies including Hershey's, AmerisourceBergen, Emerson Electric, JVC, The Michael C. Fina Company, and more. Miletsky is a featured speaker for numerous companies and seminars as well as a guest lecturer for universities. He is the author of 10 books, including *Perspectives on Marketing* and *Perspectives on Branding*, and he blogs regularly at jaymiletsky.com and getperspectives.com. You can follow him on Twitter at http://twitter.com/jaymiletsky.

CONTENTS

INTRODUCTION

In most books like this one, the author starts by saying something like "Congratulations! By deciding to open your own company, you've taken the first step into the exciting world of entrepreneurship!" Well, I'm sorry, but I can't say that. I believe you don't congratulate someone when they decide to go to college; you congratulate them four years later, when they've actually earned their degree. You don't give someone a high five for talking about climbing a mountain; you make a big deal out of it when they reach the summit. So I'm not going to congratulate you just yet.

Too many people like to talk about starting their own company—but never get any farther than that. Simply talking about something is the easy part; it doesn't accomplish anything. But actually starting your own company—really committing yourself to it—will be one of the most powerful, important decisions you'll ever make, literally altering the course of your entire life.

My entire adult life has been centered around growing my company, which I began in 1994 after graduating from Brandeis University. During my freshman year in college, I drew a "Happy Birthday" card for my girlfriend, Lisa. She showed it to a bunch of her friends, who asked me to draw cards for them to give to their friends. Before I knew it, I was selling hand-drawn greeting cards. Not enough to make any real money, but enough to make me think that I could start a greeting-card company of my own. And that's exactly what I did. Using money that I saved from waiting tables, I had 18 different card designs professionally printed, ordered envelopes and business cards, and hit the streets in my attempt to become the next Hallmark.

Of course, it wasn't quite that easy. After a few weeks of very few sales, I started to feel discouraged. Somehow, my card designs weren't impressing store owners as much as they had impressed a handful of college students. Eventually, though, I brought my cards to Vander Platt Funeral Home, thinking maybe they could sell the "I'm Sorry" designs as condolence cards. The owner of the funeral home, a very nice guy named Henry Vander Platt, didn't think he'd be able to sell the cards, but said that he needed a small brochure for the cemetery his company owned. With no other real opportunities, I quickly agreed to design his brochure.

Of course, I had never actually designed a brochure before and had no idea how to do it, but I dove in. I used an $8 throw-away camera (remember, this was 1994—not a lot of digital cameras at the time) to take some pictures of the cemetery. Writing the copy was a bit trickier; I didn't have a computer, so I created a fake student ID to gain access to the computer lab at Ramapo Valley College to write the text. Then I used scissors and Scotch tape to create a sample of the brochure for Mr. Vander Platt to approve. I also quoted a price of roughly $10,000 (not including printing) for my design. "Is this price fair?" he asked during our meeting. I really had no idea what the going rate of a small brochure was, but I had come to believe that $10,000 was a good price, so I assured him that it was. He wrote me a check for half that, with the balance to be paid when I delivered the final product. And that was that: I was out of the greeting-card business and into marketing! (I've since learned that the brochure probably should have gone for about $1,500, not $10,000. It took me a long time to realize that Mr. Vander Platt probably knew that all along and simply wanted to help out a young kid who was scrapping to launch his own company. He taught me an important lesson: As anxious as I was to make it on my own, help is sometimes necessary.)

In the years that followed, I dove headfirst into the marketing industry—an industry in which I had no previous experience or knowledge. I took clients wherever I could find them. Many of my early clients were companies with whom my dad put me in touch, others were customers I spoke with while waiting tables, and still others I acquired by making cold calls. I'd be lying if I said that those early years were fun. They weren't. They were constant work, constant stress, and constant pressure.

Over time, the business grew. After pairing up—and ultimately parting ways with—with a number of business partners, I finally joined ranks with a very talented, very business-minded partner, who has been by my side since 1999. We hired employees, then hired more employees, and eventually needed a larger office. Clients changed from small mom-and-pop stores paying $50 for business-card designs to *Fortune* 500 companies signing six-figure advertising contracts. And through it all, while the company grew and the stakes went up, one thing remained the same: The amount of work and dedication required never wavered. My company was and still is always with me, no matter what I'm doing. Although most people can separate work life from social life, for the entrepreneur, these areas are inextricably intertwined—and we wouldn't have it any other way.

If you've ever watched the last episode of the TV show *Cheers*, you've seen a testament to this very spirit. After 11 years of chasing women only to find himself still alone, Sam leaves the bar to move to the West Coast with Diane. He makes it as far as the plane before turning around and heading back to the bar. "You can never be unfaithful to your one true love," Norm says. "You always come back to her." Sam asks, "Who is that?" And Norm replies, "Think about it, Sam." Of course, he's talking about the bar. More than all his friends and all the women he dated, Sam's one true love was his business.

In hindsight, building my business probably would have been easier if I had chosen a different path. I could have tried to raise more money before getting started. I could have spent a few years in a job first, making some connections and getting an education about how the industry works. But even through the rockiest parts, I've never regretted it. Not for a moment. And that's what it's all about. Building your own company isn't like any other job. It isn't about the money, the vacations, or the freedom. It's about freeing the beast inside you that always needs to be moving forward, that always wants to win.

I wish I could tell you that my journey was an easy road or even that the rough patches weren't so hard to get through, but I can't. Chances are, your road will be difficult as well. But it will also be fulfilling, exciting, and ultimately the only endeavor that will satisfy the true entrepreneur.

What You'll Find In This Book

In this book, I've put together what I think are the important points you should consider when starting and building your business. These aren't points that I've read in other books like this one and simply rewritten to fit my own style; each of the tips I've provided have come from years of hard work and personal experience as an entrepreneur.

The book is broken up into distinct sections, organizing all points by topic. It's not linear; there's no reason to read the tips in order. It's just as effective if you jump around and read whichever section you find most interesting.

While many of the tips I've provided in this book have a practical bent, such as dealing with financial issues, marketing your company, sales, and working with business partners and employees, other sections focus more squarely on the emotional issues with which many entrepreneurs contend. These include the difficulty (but necessity) of being honest with yourself, the importance of keeping yourself sane, and how to deal with the sense of isolation that often comes with being the boss.

You'll also notice that I have somewhat of a sarcastic writing style and try to keep many of my tips lighthearted. The subject matter is important, but I wanted to create a book that would also be fun to read.

Who Should Read This Book

This book is written for anybody who is seriously considering starting his or her own business, as well as for seasoned entrepreneurs who are ready to take their company to the next level. This book is also for entrepreneurs who have a few years under their belt but would benefit from seeing how someone else has built his business, even if it's only for the purposes of knowing that other people have dealt with similar hurdles. But most of all, this book is for people with an entrepreneurial spirit who have always dreamed of running their own business and want to explore how to make that dream a reality.

Contacting the Author

If you have any questions or comments, you can reach me through e-mail at jmiletsky@getperspectives.com.

Good luck!

Part I

Things to Consider

So here you are, considering starting your own business. Maybe you've always had an entrepreneurial spirit and are finally taking the leap into small-business ownership. Or maybe the economy has taken its toll and you've boldly decided to take the bull by the horns and become the master of your own destiny. Whatever your reasons, if you're like most entrepreneurs, your mind is cluttered with images of large paychecks, vacations, and adoring, devoted employees. Before you get too lost in fantasyland, there are a few things you ought to know about starting your own company.

1. Be Honest with Yourself

One of the most important qualities entrepreneurs possess can also be one of their biggest downfalls: passion. Passion is a wonderful trait that will see you though the hard times (there will be plenty) and keep you pushing to succeed even against incredibly difficult odds. You'll need it; no business can be started without a deep passion for winning, growing, and knowing you've accomplished something.

At the same time, don't let that passion cloud your judgment. Throughout this book, there will be tips and suggestions that will require you to take a good, hard look at your business situation, your potential customers, your own capabilities, and more. Be honest with yourself at all points. Too often, entrepreneurs allow their passion and desire to grow a business get in the way of their ability to see reality—and paying a dire price for it in the end.

1

Consider these sobering 2007 statistics from SCORE (Senior Core of Retired Executives):

- There were 637,100 new businesses, 560,300 business closures, and 28,322 bankruptcies. 49,000 lasted
- Two-thirds of new employer firms survive at least two years; 44 percent survive at least four years; and 31 percent survive at least seven years.

No, that doesn't mean that you should throw in the towel, return this book, and begin searching the job boards instead. But it does mean that you're going to need to be as realistic as possible to keep from becoming a statistic.

Honesty also touches on the quality of your vision. Do you have one, or do you just have a fantasy? Let me explain the difference:

- A vision is knowing what type of work you want to do: the services you want to provide, the type of clients you want to work with, and how you see your company growing.

- A fantasy is seeing yourself on the deck of your yacht, surrounded by beautiful people as you cruise the lagoons of your own private island.

Which one are you really focused on? Once again, be honest with yourself. Because the truth is, fantasy is wonderful, but it won't get you very far.

Being honest with yourself on key issues doesn't necessarily mean your dreams of running your company will grind to a permanent halt. It just means that you'll have a better idea of what you're up against and be able to take the appropriate steps to grow the right way.

2. It Won't Be Easy

Thinking about building your own company is tons of fun! After all, imagination has a wonderful way of painting an idyllic picture. In no time, you're Gordon Gekko—brick phone and all—barking orders from your lavish penthouse office with its glass walls and leather couches. And talking about building your own company is even more fun! You walk around with your chest puffed out, telling people all about how big your company is going to be, how you're going to get great new clients. It's riveting! No doubt you'll find yourself the center of attention, suddenly vaulted to a higher level of society, commanding the respect of a seasoned CEO from everyone you talk to.

It's all fiction, of course, because you haven't actually *done* anything yet—but that doesn't stop millions of people from talking a big game. It's fun to play entrepreneur. There's no risk, no hard work…nothing but the benefits of being an executive in your own private theater. Unfortunately, there's also no reward. The fact is, actually starting and building your own company is much different from simply talking about it. Getting a successful business off the ground is extraordinarily hard work. It will take its toll on you physically, mentally, and emotionally. Will that ease? Of course it will—later. Much later. But at least for the first few years, you should expect to break your back trying to move the mountain.

To give you an idea of what that could entail, I'll reference my own humble beginnings, when I launched my company back in 1994. I was right out of college and had decided, pretty much on a whim, to start my own marketing agency. No experience, no real money of my own, and an economics degree from Brandeis University—which said plenty about my ability to put together supply-and-demand diagrams but very little about my abilities to develop advertising and marketing strategies. Using the money I had saved from my summer job, I bought my first computer, rented a small office about 15 minutes away from home (living with my parents, I quickly realized that making business calls was difficult, what with my mother vacuuming in the background), and found out from some friends in the industry that I would need to learn how to use certain graphic-design programs to develop projects such as brochures and print ads for my future clients. Not the ideal situation, but I was a one-man show after all, and I'd have to do the sales and the production all by myself.

I woke up every day at 8:00 a.m., got ready, and made it to my office by 9:00. I spent all day calling anybody I could think of to try and drum up business. I had dreams of producing national TV commercials and creating award-winning ad campaigns for Pepsi and Nike, but there I was, pandering to Joe's Plumbing Service to design their business cards and letterhead. You have to start somewhere! I made these long, exhausting, and somewhat humiliating calls until 4:00 p.m. (with a small break for a cheap lunch and a few minutes to flirt with one of the girls who worked down the hall), at which point I closed down shop and headed over to the Macaroni Grill, where I worked at nights as a waiter so I could earn some money. I ran around bringing hot plates to demanding customers for five hours; afterward, at around 11:00 p.m., I headed right back to my office, where I sat at my computer and taught myself how to do graphic design and build Web sites. Around 2:00 a.m., I headed back home to get a few hours of sleep before doing it all over again the next day.

That went on for two years. Good times.

Today, 16 years later, my agency is a thriving company with a great partner; employees handling design, account, and project management; public relations; bookkeeping; and sales. Was it worth it? Absolutely! But getting here took years of non-stop work, non-stop stress, and tunnel vision. Your own path may be more or less difficult than mine—you may have more money to start with, you may have some big clients lined up before you even open your doors—but no matter what your situation is, starting your own company will be a grind in the early years, and much much harder than simply talking about it.

3. Don't Be Too Quick to Quit Your Day Job

Don't get involved in your business full-time (in other words, don't quit your day job) until you know exactly what kind of business you want to start and you're financially prepared to make the leap. If you're like many entrepreneurs, your imagination is filled with thoughts of wealth and prosperity. Imagination is a wonderful thing, but the reality is it's just not that easy—and the early days especially can be a financial struggle. The pressure of needing to grow quickly because you lack steady income can make it difficult to make the right decisions. The one thing that your company will need as much as it needs money is time; if you have to work an additional job to ease the financial pressures on yourself, do it, and build your company gradually in the off hours.

To that end, consider either starting a company that you can run in the off hours (starting a graphic-design company, for example, would allow you to work on design projects at night while still holding down a day job) or get a job that allows you to work at night so you can concentrate on your new venture during the day.

I was right out college when I started my company and spent six nights a week waiting tables to make some extra cash while I was getting started. The bigger benefit, of course, was the built-in audience that I had: I told every person I waited on that I was starting my own company, and left everyone a business card when I gave them their check. Many of my company's early clients were people that I met while waiting tables.

4. Don't Break Your Arm Patting Yourself on the Back

Don't fool yourself into thinking that you have the greatest, most unique idea since some caveman figured out that twigs and leaves could burn. Chances are, you don't. Even if all your friends tell you that it's a great idea, the reality is that they probably just don't want to hurt your feelings. Be realistic: Buying too heavily into your own hype can lead you to make reckless decisions.

It's also not always necessary to have a unique idea around which to build a company. It's perfectly reasonable to start a company based on improving an existing idea or even just to provide another service or product option in addition to the options that are already out there. For example, if you're an accountant, you don't need to have a new idea to open a thriving accounting business—it could be enough just to open your business in an area where there's a demand for what you do and consistently perform your services well.

Innovation is wonderful, but not always necessary to be a successful entrepreneur.

5. Don't Expect Overnight Riches

Look for good opportunities to get into business or increase your company's revenue, but don't fall for stupid cons. Anything that promises overnight success or tremendous wealth without needing any talent is most likely a scam.

Multilevel marketing is also pretty ridiculous, as is anything that starts its pitch by asking you what you would do with a million dollars. Success takes time, hard work, and ingenuity; anyone who tells you anything different is just trying to rip you off.

More specifically:

- Be wary of any company that advertises in crappy magazines or whose claims seem too good to be true.
- Watch out for "testimonials" in ads that are signed Larry M., Canton OH. Giving a last-name initial is a hint that the testimonial is completely fictionalized.
- If an ad tells you that its opportunity will make your rich, but the ad itself is either black and white or half a page, ask yourself: If they're so successful, why can't they afford a color ad or a full page?
- Look for grammatical errors in "opportunity" ads, and don't be fooled by pictures of luxury cars, boats, or mansions.
- Don't ever send money to a P.O. box.

Interestingly, when I was writing this book, I visited the Small Business section of a local bookstore to get a sense of what other authors had to say on this topic. As I was looking at the various titles, a guy standing next to me asked if I was interested in starting my own company—a fair question, considering what books I was looking at. I told him I already owned my own company, but I was doing some research for a book I was writing. He nodded. "I also own my own company," he said, explaining that *his* company helped people make more money. He then asked, with a particularly ridiculous grin, "Wouldn't you like to have another $5,000 each month?" Here was a guy in his late 20s, wearing a baseball hat, an untucked flannel shirt, and old, dirty sneakers, telling me, a complete stranger in the middle of a bookstore, that he could help me earn an extra $5,000 per month.

Apparently, my knowledge or experience in, well, *anything* didn't matter. I could get some extra cash simply because that was his job. Obviously, I thought, if he could do that for me, then he must be able to do that for himself many times over! So I asked what kind of car he drove, assuming, naturally, that someone who makes the kind of money that he makes must surely have a nice car. I was right—he said he drove a Lexus, one of the more expensive models. I asked if we could go out and see it, so I could be sure he was legit. He hesitated, and explained that his Lexus was at home. He had driven his girlfriend's Honda Civic to the bookstore.

Of course he had.

The point isn't to look down on people who don't have fancy cars. My mom drives a Honda Civic—they're great cars. Rather, it's to look carefully at any opportunities that are presented to you. Take a critical approach and really analyze what makes sense and what doesn't. Your money, time, and confidence are at stake with every decision. Don't let fly-by-night scams con you out of them!

6. You Are Never, Ever Alone

For some reason, entrepreneurs love to think that their business is so exceptional that they don't have any competition. Wrong. If you believe that, you're in for a rude awakening. You absolutely *do* have competition; consumers will always have a choice between your company and an alternative.

But just accepting that competition is out there is only part of the battle. You need to do some research and really get to know them:

■ Who are they?

■ What do they do?

■ What do they offer that you don't?

■ How much of a lock do your competitors have on your potential customers and how tough will it be for you to lure those customers away?

■ Who are the key executives and what are their reputations and qualifications in the industry?

Check out their Web sites, read their blogs, see what they're about and understand what they're doing to reach their market. Armed with that information, you can pinpoint weaknesses in their products or services, differentiate your company, and ultimately improve your own sales and marketing efforts.

7. Multitasking Is a Necessary Evil

In the early stages of running your business, you're going to have to wear many hats. You'll be the president, the janitor, the secretary, the marketing director, and the sales team. If you don't think you can handle all of these roles, then think twice before you actually go into business for yourself.

8. Cash-Strapped? Consider Starting a Service Company

There's nothing wrong with boot-strapping it when you get started; that's often the entrepreneurial way of life. But if funds are low, consider launching a service business, such as one involving child care, house cleaning, accounting, consulting, or something along those lines, rather than a product-oriented one. Service businesses are usually cheaper to start and build because there's less overhead at the outset (no manufacturing or financial outlay for materials) and you won't have to keep and store inventory.

9. Inexperience Isn't Necessarily a Negative

Want to know a sure-fire way to *not* get a job with my marketing agency? Come to an interview and give me the textbook answer to any marketing-related question I ask. Thanks, but no thanks. I can read books, too. What I'm looking for are employees who can think on their own and come up with unique solutions to common problems, not people who can regurgitate standard-issue responses.

The same goes for starting a business. There are instances when experience can be helpful, saving time and money. But that doesn't mean that experience alone can provide necessary solutions, nor does it mean that having experience is the best way to succeed. In fact, in many instances, experience could be a hindrance, keeping you from thinking outside the proverbial box.

I like to tell people that part of the reason my own company grew in the early years was that with many of the decisions I made, I was simply too stupid to know any better. I went after large clients that more experienced people in my industry told me not to bother with, saying my agency was too small and wouldn't get any attention. I developed creative advertising concepts for clients that other people with years of marketing experience advised me against—but that ultimately proved successful. Fortunately, I was too stupid to know any better, which kept my mind free enough to make my own decisions.

Obviously, that's not to say you'll make worse decisions for your company as you gain more experience. Clearly that's not the case. As you grow your company, the experience you gain will help you make wise choices and likely propel you to grow even faster. But that doesn't mean it's absolutely necessary when you get your company started. If you have an idea or a passion to do something that you've never done before, go for it. The experience will come later.

10. Go Ahead and Share Your Ideas

If you're reluctant to tell anybody about your ideas for fear that they might be stolen, stop worrying. Nobody is going to quit what they're currently doing so they can steal your idea and run with it. (Chances are it sounds a lot better in your own head than it does in someone else's ears.) Eventually, you're going to have to tell *somebody* what your idea is, whether it's a banker, a lawyer, a potential investor, etc. Is there a chance that the idea will get stolen? There's always a chance—but it's a long shot. If you're really concerned, you could have an NDA (non-disclosure agreement) drafted and signed by anybody you present your ideas to, but those can be tough to enforce—and unless you have a good amount of industry cred behind you, you'll find many people reluctant to sign it.

11. Survival Relies on Market Need

Consider the potential market you can service with a new company before you get too involved. Make sure that a market or a need for your service exists. If you want to open a typewriter-repair shop, for example, chances are you're going to be running a very lonely company.

For your company to survive and prosper, at least one of the following must exist:

- Genuine need (such as food, shoes, etc.) that is not being filled to capacity
- Perceived need (handbags, "fad" items, cleaning services, etc.)
- The ability to improve upon existing products or services or provide them more inexpensively

If there's no demand for what you're selling or the demand is already being met by other companies that do it better and/or cheaper, then you may want to ask yourself (before you invest too heavily) if there is really room for you in the market.

One of the biggest hurdles in determining whether there's a market need for what you want to sell was discussed in the very first point of this book: being honest with yourself. When you have your heart set on starting a new company, it can be very difficult to accurately and honestly look at a market and say "Well, there's just no room for me here." We all want to believe that other people will be as passionate about our company as we are. Admitting otherwise is almost like accepting defeat before you even get started.

Once, I came home from college during winter break to the small town in northern New Jersey where I grew up, and was surprised to find that a new, independent brass-bed store had opened near the local grocery. It seemed odd and out of place—apart from the fact that the town was relatively small, we were only about 10 miles away from two very large malls and a highway flanked on either side by well-known furniture stores. How high could the demand for brass beds be, and why would people who needed them buy them from this store when so many other options were available? When I came back from college the next summer, the brass-bed store was already gone, replaced by a florist.

I understand what the proprietors of the brass-bed store were think-ing. They had an idea, they somehow had access to inventory, and they talked themselves into believing that there was demand. They must have known about the nearby malls and the larger furniture stores, and they must have realized that brass beds aren't something that anyone needs to buy very often, but in their love for their own business, they convinced themselves that local people would support a local business and they'd be a success. Unfortunately, they wasted a lot of time and money to find out the truth the hard way—as do many other entrepreneurs who improperly analyze the true need for their products and services. Don't fall into that trap, and don't allow your emotions, excitement, and passion to get the best of you.

12. You'll Need to Be a Risk Taker

One trait shared by many entrepreneurs is a propensity for gambling. I'm not saying we're all going to be lined up outside Gamblers Anonymous, but I haven't met another business owner yet who didn't enjoy going to a casino, jumping into a poker game, hitting a racetrack, or participating in a football pool every now and then. That's because we're all gamblers at heart, willing to take a risk to make it big. Risk is inherent in starting any business—you're putting up your own money in the hope that it will give you a positive return, while recognizing that there's no guarantee of that, and that it's very likely you could lose all of it.

If you want safe, put your money in a long-term CD and get a job with a solid company. You'll know exactly how much you'll make by the end of the year. And while your upward growth will be limited, so will your risk; as long as you don't lose your job, you're safe. But if you want something more—if you want a shot at real success—then be prepared to take a significant risk.

Taking risks when it comes to building a business means going all out from beginning to end. The worst thing you can do is let up in the middle. At some point, however, that's likely to be a consideration. Chances are you'll find that the entire venture was more expensive than you had originally expected, and you'll get scared and be tempted to pull back. Unless you're in dire financial straits, stick with the initial course and don't back away from the risk.

Years ago, I had a business partner who considered himself a risk-taker but was really quite conservative. That became very apparent (and was the beginning of the end of our business relationship) when we had the opportunity to handle a large marketing account for Washington Mutual that would likely gross us about $1,000,000 over the course of the next year.

On the surface, it sounded like a solid opportunity, but there was actually significant risk involved. From the moment we received the call that we had gotten the account, we were expected to get started. But getting started would cost us more than $100,000—and like most large companies, Washington Mutual didn't pay deposits, and paid invoices on a net 30 basis from the date the invoice is processed (which could be two weeks after it's sent). Worse yet, the working contract still had to be written and approved—which would be at least a month—during which time there'd be nothing but a handshake to keep the client from backing out of the whole deal. And because we didn't have $100,000 lying around, we would need to borrow it from a bank, which meant putting up our homes and other belongings as collateral.

So the risk was our homes, but the potential reward was our first million-dollar account with what was at the time the biggest bank in the country. I voted to take the risk; my partner voted not to. Eventually, I won that battle, and Washington Mutual went on to become one of our largest clients for the next five years—but I lost a business partner in the process,

As any good gambler will tell you, the two keys to winning are to be consistent and to take calculated risks. This tip shouldn't be interpreted as a suggestion to be reckless; rather, it should be a confirmation that the smart risks you do take are a necessary part of growing your business.

13. Do What You Love, But Put the Barbed-Wire Collection Away

You may be tempted to build your business from your hobby. It's not a bad idea, but depending on what your hobby is, it may be hard to turn a profit by making a company out of it. It might be hard to find a market for your collection of barbed wire. Even if there is a market—for example, if you want to sell baseball cards—you might face stiff competition from others who are willing to sacrifice profit for their love of the hobby.

All that being said, you should do something you love. Just look for an angle that allows you to do it and make money at it at the same time. In my case, I loved the artistic process of coming up an initial idea and bringing it to life, but I wasn't prepared to be a starving artist. I also didn't want to work for minimal freelance rates. So I honed my skills and built an advertising agency that gave me greater security and increased credibility, and still allowed me to exist right in the middle of an artistic industry.

14. Be Prepared: There Are Tons of Unexpected Costs

Be realistic about your start-up finances. How much money do you actually have with which to start your company? Be truthful with yourself, because tons of expenses are going to pop up that you won't anticipate or expect, and you're going to need some cash to cover them. Sure, lots of companies start out on a shoestring budget, but if you underestimate how many unexpected costs you'll face, you may find yourself in a hole that you can't dig yourself out of.

It's always better to be conservative in your estimations when calculating your expenses. For example, suppose you price out a computer at $1,195, so you budget $1,200 for computer expenses. But did you account for the sales tax? The accessories that you'll be tempted to buy? If you're the naïve type, you might even spend another $150 on the extended warranty. And what about the software you're going to need and people you may have to hire to help you set up your Internet connection? Did you consider the back-up hard drive to make sure you don't lose any of your important files? By the time you plug the thing in, you've spent far more than expected on a computer for which you originally budgeted only $1,200.

The same goes for client projects. Often, especially in service companies, certain costs of doing business are overlooked to keep prices low. It's easy to estimate how many hours a project will take you, and prices quoted to the client are often based on that figure. But there will likely be hard costs that come into play. Maybe you'll find that you need to hire a freelancer to help with part of the project. Or maybe you're going to need to buy specific materials that you hadn't considered, or you end up running late getting something to the client and need to send it overnight. All these things cost money, and all of them will eat into your profit. So if you expected to make $5,000, you suddenly might find you've only made $4,000. It ends up being a big difference, especially in the early days when every dollar really counts.

It's easy to underestimate costs because we always want to paint the most positive picture for our business that we can. Entrepreneurs are famous for fooling themselves into believing that their finances are better than they really are. Avoid that temptation. Being realistic about costs will keep you in business a lot longer. Everything is more expensive than we anticipate. It's the way the world works, so prepare yourself. Always round expenses up and always keep an eye out for unexpected costs.

15. Some Key Skills Are Absolutely Necessary

As the owner of your company, the success of your business will rest on your shoulders as a businessperson, salesperson, and as president and CEO. To achieve this success, you'll need to possess or quickly develop the following three things:

- **Good writing skills.** This may not be super important if, say, you own a bakery. But for most non-retail businesses, you'll be expected to do a lot of writing—probably more than you realize. In particular, e-mails will take up a good amount of time as you start to increase your list of clients and potential clients—and while e-mail is often pretty informal, you're going to want to dial the professionalism up a notch when e-mailing clients. You'll also potentially be writing long proposals. These should be anything but informal. In addition to providing a price, they should also help sell the product or service. Your company's

brochures and Web-site content will also need to be written—
and unless you want to spend the money to have a marketing
agency or professional copywriter do it for you, you can
expect to get out your literary pen for these, too. These are
just a few examples of materials that require different types of
writing, and you could very well be the author for each of
them. Learning to write well is a must.

■ **An expanded vocabulary with proper grammatical skills.**
The fastest way to sound like an idiot is to butcher the
English language. Conversely, the best way to leave people
with the impression that you're intelligent is to use the
language well. I'm not saying you need to have a vocabulary
that rivals Dennis Miller's, but dropping a few $5 words now
and then can go a long way.

■ **The ability to speak well in public.** When people think
about public speaking, they most often imagine being on stage,
looking into large room packed with hundreds of unforgiving
faces ready to heckle them at the first hint of insecurity or a
mistake. In truth, those situations really aren't as bad as all
that—although it's one of the things people fear the most,
public speaking is often worse in our imaginations than it is in
reality—but large seminar speaking isn't the type of speaking
you'll really need to concern yourself with. Although being a
featured speaker at large events may one day figure into your
marketing plans, as you begin your company, the type of
speaking you'll *really* need to master centers on client meetings and presentations, as well as meeting new people at
networking events. These will be important forums for selling
yourself and your company, and the future of both can rest on
the words you use and the way you use them.

You can improve your writing abilities and expand your vocabulary
by reading more. Many entrepreneurs are so anxious to get right to
work that they feel doing anything not directly tied to their company
is a waste of time. But reading anything—particularly books, magazines, or blog posts that focus on your industry—will not only keep
you in the know and up-to-date about what other people in your
world are doing, but it will help you become a better writer and
expand your vernacular. Speaking well in public, on the other hand,

usually requires some practice. Rehearse in front of a mirror, friend, or family member. When I first started my company I practiced upcoming client presentations by collecting a bunch of stuffed animals and action figures and setting them up around a conference table.

No, I'm not embarrassed to admit that....

16. Nothing Slows Life Down Like a Committee

Making decisions by committee is the death of progress. Anyone whose opinion you ask will feel it's necessary to change something or to somehow put his or her fingerprints on the decision. Forget that. It's a waste of time. Don't ask opinions from people who aren't directly associated with your business. Most often, the real reason entrepreneurs seek the advice of their hair stylist, neighbor, mailman, or dog is because they're trying to do a little showing off. It once again goes back to the difference between *being* a CEO and *playing* one.

One of the most important talents needed to be a business owner is the ability to make strong, firm decisions. By taking the helm of your company, you're talking a leadership role—and that means taking charge and accepting responsibility for the outcome and consequences. Often, you'll need to make decisions quickly and without a lot of information in front of you. You'll have to act on instinct. Sometimes you'll make the right decision, sometimes you'll make the wrong one. Accept ownership of them all.

Don't allow yourself to be greatly swayed by the thoughts and opinions of other people around you—especially if they aren't directly involved with your business. Other people don't have the benefit of your insight, and they may have other priorities in mind. For example, suppose you're considering putting your home up as collateral against a loan in order to make a bigger investment in your company. While you might see the potential, friends and family members who are more risk averse and likely to play it safe may advise you against it.

If you need to consult with others—brainstorming isn't a bad thing—pick one or maybe two people you trust to really listen to you and give you sound feedback. That's a happy medium, giving you access to other frames of thoughts without opening important decisions up to a random committee. But no matter who you consult, their perspectives and sensibilities will differ from yours; ultimately, *you're* the one who has to live with the decisions that you make. So make them.

17. The Truth Behind Being Your Own Boss

The term "you're your own boss" is very comforting to most entrepreneurs. They're the king. The head honcho. No boss means nobody to push them around. Isn't that what everyone wants?

Apparently it is. I often guest-lecture at area colleges, speaking to students in entrepreneurship classes. Most of the students have a sincere interest in starting their own company after graduation. I always start off by asking the question: Why? Not surprisingly, "I want to be my own boss" is always an answer.

On the surface, it does sound ideal. We've all seen TV shows that exaggerate an angry, abusive boss (my personal favorite being Mr. Spacely of Spacely Space Sprockets, George Jetson's boss on *The Jetsons*), and maybe we've had our own personal experiences with bosses who didn't treat us well. But before you assume that being your own boss is a good thing, let's look at it a little more carefully.

To begin with, are you *really* your own boss? Sure, you own the company, and there's nobody above you to whom you have report. There's also nobody to fire you, tell you to pack up your desk, and escort you out to your car. So in that sense, sure, you won't have a boss. That perception changes, though, as soon as an angry clients calls, screaming into the phone that the project you're doing is taking too much time or that they're unhappy with a service you've provided and threaten to take their account elsewhere. They say "Jump," you say "How high?" And that's when you realize that quite the opposite of not having a boss at all, you have many bosses—each and every one of your clients. And these people can be every bit as cutting and belittling as any "real" boss could ever be.

There's also the question of freedom. As the boss of the company, you have one great advantage over people who are employees: Employees can get fired, and you can't. The flip side of that is that they can quit, and you can't. For most people who simply work for a company, leaving requires little more than saying "I quit" and walking out. As your own boss, you don't have that luxury. If you don't love what you do—owning and running a company for the sheer excitement of owning and running a company in good times and bad—well, you'll be out of luck, because unraveling the whole thing and shutting the company down can be a long and winding road.

Think carefully about the downsides of being your own boss before making the ultimate decision to take that route. While it's easy to associate that position with absolute freedom, the reality is that it can be anything but.

18. "Clever" Often Outsmarts "Smart"

Within a month of opening my Facebook account, I was reconnected with about 90 percent of my high-school graduating class. While I didn't necessarily feel a need to start chatting with everyone, it was interesting to see what they had all been up to since leaving Indian Hills High School in 1990, and I was able to confirm for myself a thesis I had formulated a long time ago: Book-smarts didn't necessarily go hand in hand with entrepreneurial success. In fact, most of the people who graduated near the top of my class ended up as doctors, lawyers, or in middle-management positions. As far as I could tell, there were no business owners among them. Not that that's a bad thing—it's just interesting. Because while there are plenty of examples of people with book-smarts who opened very successful businesses (Bill Gates seems to have done okay for himself), by and large, achieving success is more a question of being clever than being smart.

I first learned this lesson in the early days of my marketing agency. I was sitting in my office—a 10×10-foot box that I rented in a building packed with other 10×10-foot businesses—making cold calls for new business when I realized how many hurdles were actually in my path. I was fresh out of college with an economics degree that meant nothing to anybody who would hire my company for marketing, I had no marketing experience, and I had no portfolio of past work to show anybody.

Moving forward in any situation is a matter of problem solving: analyzing the issues you're faced with and figuring out a way around them, like a large, never-ending game of chess. So my personal challenge was very clear: How do I get other companies to hire my company without wanting to see a portfolio of past work—and without concentrating on my lack of marketing experience? The answer was simple: Make it all about them, and not about me. So I collected local magazines and newspapers, went through the ads, and called companies who had advertised, no matter how large or small. I'd get the marketing director on the phone, introduce myself, and say, "I saw your ad in [insert name of magazine here], and while I thought it was a good ad [I'd never put the ad down—that would make them defensive], I thought it might be a bit more effective with a different layout. I've already taken the liberty to redesign the ad, and was wondering if I could come by and show you what I've done with it?"

The key was to say that I had already redesigned the ad. Of course I hadn't, but they didn't need to know that. By saying I had, I piqued their interest; they were curious to see what I had done. Seven times out of 10, I'd get a meeting, which I'd schedule for two weeks later; in that time, I'd redesign their ad, making sure it was better than the one they had originally published. More often than, not they'd like what I showed them, and they'd give me a starter project, like a small brochure to design for them. And they'd almost never ask me to present a portfolio of work I had done for other companies. Why would they? I had already showed them what I could do for *their* company.

Mission accomplished on all fronts. As you grow your own company, look for creative ways to solve problems. The answer usually relies on being more clever than smart.

19. Be Dedicated or Be Out of Business

How dedicated are you to owning a company? If the answer is less than 100 percent, then you should get a job instead. Don't know how to measure 100 percent? Ask yourself the following questions:

- What are your final thoughts before you fall asleep at night?
- What goes through your mind as you are eating? Relaxing?
- What do you think about while you're driving? In the shower? Having a drink with a friend?

If your answer is, "I think about how to grow my company," then congratulations. You're at the 100-percent mark.

That might seem a bit extreme, but so is entrepreneurship. This isn't a career for wimps—it's a lifestyle that has to become part of you. You have to live, breathe, and love it like it's your child, because in many ways it will be. You created it, gave it life, and are responsible for helping it grow. It will take all your attention and effort to make sure it grows up right.

Part 2

Getting Started

Aren't the beginnings always the hardest? Getting out of bed in the morning, getting started on a new exercise regimen, going on a first date and trying to not look like an idiot by trying too hard to just be yourself…. Very few people really enjoy beginnings, and fewer still deal with them well.

Starting your company may be one of the toughest beginnings of them all. Where do you start? How do you start? There are so many variables, it can seem like an insurmountable undertaking. The following points touch on a few of the many issues you may wonder about as you get your business started—and a few issues you probably never even thought of.

20. Retain the Two Most Important People First

As soon as you decide to open your own business, the first thing you need to do is hire a lawyer and an accountant/financial advisor to guide you as your company grows. Even if you think legal and financial stuff should be pretty simple and that common sense would dictate, it's almost never the case. Having a good lawyer and a good accountant could save you from making costly mistakes.

The very first job your lawyer should handle for you is the registration process for your company (especially if it's going to be any type of corporation) to ensure the legality of the business. The lawyer should also do a name search to confirm that the name that you want is available. If you're doing it on your own as a sole proprietorship or a partnership, then make sure you register the company with the proper agencies in your town, district, county, or state. Although it's possible to do the initial setup yourself, most lawyers won't charge much for this service. It's worthwhile to let them do it and make sure it gets done correctly.

21. Free Labor Is Never Free, So Avoid It at All Costs

Although these tips are not necessarily meant to be read one right after another, I think it's appropriate and important to put this entry right after the one about hiring a lawyer and an accountant as one of your first priorities. The early days of getting a company started are among the most important—and the most volatile. As an entrepreneur, you're going to be anxious to get the drudgery of paperwork and forms out of the way and get on with the real excitement of sales and building your company. At the same time, you're also going to find out very quickly exactly how fast money will fly out of your bank account before you've even had a chance to make your first sale.

To compensate, you'll be tempted to use free labor to get things moving without having to pay anything for it. We all know an accountant or a lawyer we can tap into; many of us know one or both who we're close enough to that they'll happily help us for free. Sounds great! Only....free is *never* free. Free might not cost you actual dollars directly, but you'll pay for "free" by giving up the right to call and hound them to move faster. If you're not paying them, you lose the ability to call and ask where your files are and when everything will be completed. If they get another client in—a paying client—guess who gets pushed to the end of the line?

Saving money is great, but save it in the right places. Don't accept free services for anything that you'll be in a rush to receive or from anybody who you may need to contact and question frequently. Aggravation and potential problems will prove to be a high price to pay for "free."

22. Choose the Right Kind of Company Classification

There are four types of companies to consider:

- **Sole proprietorship.** This is the simplest type of company you can open. You will own this type of company outright, and will be solely responsible for all decisions and debts. While it's easy to get a sole proprietorship started, it's also the most financially dangerous; you'll be held personally accountable for all liabilities, and your assets (including jointly owned assets if you're married) will be at risk. You will have the right to sell the business if you decide to do so.

- **Partnership.** There are two types of partnerships to explore. A general partnership is made up of two or more co-owners. Typically, each partner splits the profits equally unless a partnership agreement is drafted beforehand. (If one partner invests significantly more money into the company, for example, a partnership agreement might be written so that the bigger investor receives more of the profits.) As with a sole proprietorship, a general partnership gives you no financial protection; you and your partner(s) will be responsible for any debt incurred by the company. The other type of partnership is a limited partnership, in which one or more general partners manage the business while a limited partner contributes funds and shares the profits. The limited partner plays no management role and has no responsibility for outstanding debt.

- **Corporation.** Once established with the state (it must be properly filed, and certain fees must be paid), a corporation becomes its own entity and is owned by its shareholders (in this case, you and any partners you may have). There are two types of corporations. A C-corporation provides the most financial protection and allows the most choices when it comes to issuing stocks and providing fringe benefits to employees. An S-corporation is for smaller companies (with no more than 75 shareholders). It offers limited financial protection and can issue only one class of stock. Many small companies opt for S-corp status because it's cheaper to open, easier to maintain, and still offers some financial protection. With any corporation, however, speak to your accountant in detail about how to deal with profits. If you're not careful, you'll end up in tax trouble. (S-corp profits get passed along to you, and you will be personally responsible for taxes on them; C-corps may be double-taxed: on profits and then again on any dividends that are paid.) As a small, new company, even if you are incorporated, you will likely be held personally responsible for company debt, as vendors may require you to personally sign for and guarantee any significant purchases or loans. You can expect that sort of practice to continue until your company has sufficient resources of its own to carry a debt safely.

- **Limited liability company.** A limited liability company (LLC) is a hybrid between a partnership and a corporation and a popular choice for many business owners. . Among the reasons for this growing popularity is the fact that LLCs limit the liability for business debt to the amount invested. They also let you choose whether you want to be treated as a partnership or as a corporation, depending on which has the lower tax burden.

Decide what kind of company to start based on what your lawyers and accountants tell you about potential tax risks and legal requirements. Chances are, if your company is large enough to be a C-corp, you wouldn't be reading this book in the first place. To protect yourself from liability, your best bets are to choose between an LLC and an S-corp. Go with an LLC if you want more flexibility and ease of operation, and go with an S-corp if you want to save on employment taxes.

23. Think Long and Hard About Your Company's Name

If you've ever tattooed the name of a girlfriend on your body only to have her break up with you a week later, you can appreciate the importance of picking the right name for your company. It's going to stay with you for a long time, so make sure you pick one that you like and will be happy living with. Here are some things to consider:

- The best names are ones that have some sort of meaning. Some people name their company after their very first pet; others create a company name by combining the last names of two more or more business partners. Still others pick a company name by reaching back into history to find a hero or personality they admire or, even more commonly, naming their company after a character from mythology. (Nike seemed to have had some success there....)

- There will be lawyers who recommend you avoid using your full name as the name of your company, such as Jay Miletsky, LLC., because it can create some issues regarding liability. If you're inclined to go the eponymous route, it's better to talk to your lawyer first.

- Don't be too literal when naming your company. In other words, don't go with "Best Accountant Ever, LLC." Many of the most successful companies are rather vague about what they do, at least when it comes to their company name. Amazon.com, not Books.com, is the leading online bookseller.

Ultimately, your company's name should reflect you, your products, and your personality, while also being memorable and easy to pronounce. And as important as it is for your market to like it, it's most important that you be happy with it because you'll be living with it for a long time.

24. Register Your Company's Name as a URL

By now, it's standard practice for any potential customer to want to check out your Web site before buying anything from your company. Having an informative, organized, and aesthetically pleasing Web site will factor heavily into your customers' view of your company.

I'll talk more about the design and development of your site later in this book. For now, concentrate on securing the best possible domain name—the part between the "www" and the ".com" in your Web address—for your company. You want to make your Web site as easy for customer to find as possible, so make sure its URL reflects your company's name.

If your exact company name isn't available, look for alternatives that are relatively close. For example, if your company's name is The Tasty Baker, then the obvious choice for a URL is www.TheTastyBaker.com. If that's taken, choose an alternative URL that doesn't stray too far from the original. You might think, "But a name is a name! If my company's name isn't available, then I'm kind of stuck." When you give it a little thought, though, you'll find there are lots of viable alternatives. You could try using dashes or underscores, as in www.The-Tasty-Baker.com or www.The_Tasty_Baker.com. Or you could try the name with the business designation attached, as in www.TheTastyBakerLLC.com. If you still don't have any luck, then try them all again, but this time add a call-to-action verb in front, such as www.GetTheTastyBaker.com or www.EatTheTastyBaker.com.

One thing you *shouldn't* do is give up on finding a .com domain and opt for .net, a .org, or anything else. While those are fine for supplemental domains, it's not wise to park your company's site on anything other than a .com domain. It's the most widely known and the most widely used; going with anything else will ultimately reduce traffic to your site.

25. Business Plans: Should You Bother?

If you're like the typical entrepreneur, you're anxious to get started and do things as quickly as possible. Preparation is no fun; you want to get going, already! This brings us to business plans: Do you or don't you need one?

For me, the determining factor is whether you'll be seeking outside financing from one or more private investors. If so, then you'll need a business plan. While I'm usually an advocate of outsourcing projects so you can concentrate on sales, in this case I think you're better off writing it on your own. For one thing, hiring someone else to write it for you can be expensive. Besides, it's your company, your passion, and your vision; no one will be able to convey that better than you can. You should be able to find some sample plans online that you can use as guideline. I've put together a list of sites that provide good sample plans on my blog, jaymiletsky.com. Check out this book's title in the Book section to locate it.

If you're not looking for financing, then I say skip the business plan. If entrepreneurship is about anything at all, it's about *doing*, not paper pushing. As the owner, you're going to need to be flexible and know when to make radical changes to the path your taking; business plans (and investors) don't always leave room for that. You're also going to know when to spend time on anything not directly related to running the business and increasing sales, and writing a business plan without the need (or desire) for investors doesn't fall into that category.

26. Legally Protect All Products and Designs

Talk to a lawyer to make sure you are filing for all the proper trademarks, patents, and copyrights that you might need to protect your company. This goes for any products that you create, systems you develop, logos you adopt for your company, etc.

A patent protects your invention. A copyright protects published and unpublished recorded work (not ideas) from authors, songwriters, poets, programmers, etc. A trademark protects goods and products, while a servicemark distinguishes services of one provider from another.

Contrary to popular myth, putting something you create in a sealed envelope and mailing it to yourself so that it has a dated postmark on the unopened envelope is not a substitute for government protection. I'm not going to bother getting too into all the different types of protection you can apply for because you really shouldn't be doing it on your own. That's what your lawyer is for. If you're aggressive and serious about growth, you'd be wise to farm out filing for protection and concentrate as much on sales and growth as possible.

27. Don't Be Caught Without Good Insurance

Consult with a risk manager or insurance broker about any insurance policies you should have for your company. Besides general liability insurance, if you have partners, you and your partners may need life insurance. (In the event of their death, you don't want to suddenly find yourself partnered to their spouses.) You might also need errors and omissions insurance (this prevents you from eating the heavy costs of any mistakes your company makes that your clients will hold you liable for) and numerous other policies to keep you protected.

Don't skip coverage or get the cheapest policy you can find; one uninsured catastrophe or lawsuit could mean the end of your business. Protect yourself as much as you possibly can. Remember: We are living in litigious times, and there are a lot of people who won't think twice about suing you for the smallest mistake. Even if you're in the right, the time and dollars you'll waste defending yourself will make you wish you had invested in decent insurance policies.

28. Image Is Everything; Pay More for It

Visual imagery will be the primary way your market makes any kind of association with your company. While the concept of "branding" deals mostly with the building of a reputation, an important part of developing the brand is creating images that will represent your company. When starting your company, these visuals will need to be an area of steady concentration.

Unfortunately, visuals are also an area where many entrepreneurs try to save a bit of money. Not realizing the importance of their image, they make the mistake of letting underqualified individuals take the reins, often trusting people who they later have a hard time providing with an honest critique such as a nephew or the son or daughter of a close friend. In extremely scary cases, entrepreneurs, under the incorrect belief that they are both creative and artistic, decide to develop the necessary visuals themselves.

I hate to break to you, but understanding how to crop an image in Photoshop doesn't make you an expert in branding or graphic design. There's far more to designing the brand visuals than simply coming up with nice images. The images must *mean* something. They have to speak to a target buyer. For example, if your primary market is female, you could easily miss the mark by using fonts and colors that are more masculine in nature. To do it right, you need to have someone who understands this and who will develop designs that will attract the right audience.

At the same time, the quality of your look will speak volumes about the professionalism, experience, and organization of your company. If the look and feel is childish and poorly executed, then there's no reason for new, potential customers to believe that they're going to get high-quality service from you.

The best idea is to outsource this work to a qualified professional. I'm not advocating that you blow a lot of money by hiring an agency—agency prices are usually too high for start-up companies—but there are plenty of marketing freelancers who can do the job at a reasonable price. In particular, look to hire qualified professionals to handle visual elements such as the logo, acceptable colors, font styles, business cards, and letterhead. I'll discuss all these and other marketing materials later in this book; for now, it's enough to emphasize the importance of visual elements as the key items for helping consumers recognize and remember your company, and that they are something in which you should invest.

29. Create a Detailed Inventory List

Figure out exactly what products or services your company will offer to customers. Create a detailed inventory on paper to get a real idea of what you're planning to sell. For example, if you're opening a bakery, it's not enough to say "I'll sell cakes and cookies." Instead, you need to make a list of everything you're planning to sell and in what quantities. If you don't, you'll have no way to create projections of costs or sales goals.

This will likely be a pretty easy exercise if you're selling a product, such as in the preceding bakery example. This gets more difficult if you're planning to build a service company. Even though I've owned my marketing agency for nearly 15 years, I still struggle to put together a comprehensive list of services that we provide. The easiest thing to do is to say we do marketing, plain and simple, and leave it at that. But that doesn't tell potential clients anything. It doesn't help them figure out whether or not we can help them. So we break down our list of services and include advertising—but even *that* ends up being vague. What does advertising entail? Is it strategy? Media planning? Creative? For print, TV, radio, all of the above? You get the point.

On the one hand, you don't want to leave anything out that could cost you an opportunity to grab some work. The worst thing in the world is to leave a service off the list, only to have a prospective client say, "Huh…too bad you don't do this one particular service. That's what I'm *really* looking for!" It's hard to backpedal and insist that you actually *do* provide that service. On the other hand, if you have too many services on your list, it could seem bloated and unrealistic—especially if you're a small company.

These issues might seem mind-numbingly boring, but at some point, you'll be expected to present your company and what you do to potential clients—and that presentation will need to be as comprehensive as possible. Give it some real thought. You'll find yourself at a disadvantage if you go into business with only a vague idea of what you're actually selling.

30. Watch Out for Hungry, Low-Flying Vultures

Suppose you're starting a small desktop-publishing business. Inevitably, you'll be approached by people who have a "unique idea—one that nobody else is doing"—say, some kind of local entertainment guide. They'll offer you part of their future revenues if you do the layout work for free.

As you start to grow, a lot of other small companies will try to barter with you. Before you accept, remember a few things:

- Theirs is not the greatest idea in the world (to anybody but them).
- It has been done before. Sorry to say it, but Joe Smith from down the street probably didn't come up with an idea that nobody else in the history of the whole world has thought of.
- You are not in the investing business (well, unless you're literally in the investing business…).

Later, when you're more established and richer, you can take a risk on some of the ideas you get approached with, but don't do it before then—no matter how great they make the offer sound.

31. The Least You'll Need to Buy

Every entrepreneur will have needs that are specific to their business. Some will need a large neon sign over the front door. Others will need an awning or a van. But there is a basic laundry list of items that pretty much every company will need, no matter what kind of business you're in. So while some of the items might seem fairly basic and obvious, the following is a list of some of the very least you'll need when you get started:

- A computer. I'm a Mac guy, and recommend Macs every chance I get. But they are a bit more expensive, so if you're looking to save money, then get yourself a PC laptop with at least the following:
    - 4GB memory
    - A quality processor (don't skimp on this, or you'll wait forever for your computer to get things done)
    - A CD and DVD player and recorder
    - A built-in WiFi card
    - A built-in camera
    - At least two USB ports
    - A 15-pin VGA video connector
    - At least a 15-inch monitor

NOTE A 13-inch monitor might look okay at the store, especially when you see the lower price points, but chances are you'll have your computer for at least two years. Give your eyes a break and go for the bigger monitor.

- Software. Depending on the computer you get, some of the software you'll need may come pre-installed. But just to be sure, here are the programs you'll need:
    - Microsoft Office. Of particular importance are Word, Excel, and PowerPoint.

NOTE At some point, Google may offer similar products online, but the idea of Web based applications like this make me uncomfortable. Google already has enough information about everyone, and I don't like the thought of relying on being able to access the Web in order to do my work. But that's just me.

- Some anti-virus program. As a Mac guy, I really couldn't tell you which one is best (Macs don't get viruses), but if you're going to get a PC, you should have one. (Personally, I think the virus-protection–software companies are probably the ones who create most of the viruses in the first place, but I have no evidence to support that. Just a theory.)

- ACT. This is a program for managing contacts and customer relationships. If you don't opt for ACT, you'll need something that does basically the same thing.

- QuickBooks. This software manages your invoicing, bank accounts, and other bookkeeping. Again, if you don't opt for QuickBooks, you'll need something that does basically the same thing and is equally powerful.

- An e-mail program. Go for Microsoft Outlook or something similar.

NOTE Although you can use gmail, Yahoo!, or some other online e-mail provider, doing so will make you look smaller. As I discuss in Part 6, "Marketing, Sales, and Dealing with Clients," you'll be better off getting a domain name and having your e-mail come to that address.

- A color printer, ink, and paper
- A scanner
- A back-up drive
- Printed and/or digital stationery. You'll need printed envelopes with your company name, logo, and return address, but you don't really need to spend money on printed letterhead, invoices, or things like that. Electronic versions of those items are fine.

- A fax machine (yes, people still use those)
- Surge protectors
- Standard office supplies. These include the following:
  - Pens
  - Pads of paper
  - Post-it® notes
  - Paper clips
  - Staplers and staples
  - Scotch tape
  - First-aid kit (especially if you're going to have employees)
  - Coffee mug (really, what desk is complete without one?)
  - Recordable CDs and/or a memory stick to easily transfer files
- A small safe to keep valuable papers and other private materials
- At least one filing cabinet, and file folders with multi-colored tabs
- Service accounts. These include the following:
  - Phone company. Do some research to determine what makes more sense economically: using a landline phone or running all calls through your cell phone.
  - Internet service provider. Get the fastest speed you can comfortably afford.
  - Federal Express, UPS, or other shipping provider
  - Outside IT manager. You probably won't need to open an account with an IT management company, but unless you know how to fix computers yourself, it'd be a good idea to know who to call in case your computers go down and you need to get something fixed in a hurry.
- A dry-erase board and/or dry-erase calendar with non-permanent markers, an eraser, and the spray stuff that supposedly cleans the board but really only works about 50 percent of the time

32. The Least (Computer Skills) You'll Need to Know

Clearly, every entrepreneur will have to have some knowledge about the industry he or she is about to jump into. In addition to that, there are certain basic pieces of information that you'll need to know, regardless of the business you're opening. (Again, some of these will seem very basic, but you'd be surprised by how many people are woefully lacking in these skills.)

- How to type. I type with two fingers, but I'm fast. Fast typists can get a lot more done in their day than slow typists. Knowing how to type includes knowing certain universal keyboard commands, such as the following:

  - Command/Ctrl+C = Copy

  - Command/Ctrl+X = Cut

  - Command/Ctrl+V = Paste

  - Command/Ctrl+P = Print

- The basics of specific software:

  - Microsoft Word (word processing)

  - Excel (spreadsheets)

  - PowerPoint (presentations)

  - ACT (customer management)

  - QuickBooks (bookkeeping)

- How to use e-mail. This will be your primary means of communication with clients, prospects, and vendors. Make sure you understand how to create a signature, how to include a hyperlink in the body of your e-mail, how to set up your address book, how and when to send a BCC, how to create folders, when to delete older e-mails (to keep your computer from slowing down or crashing), what to do if you're over quota and e-mail can't get through, and other types of info.

- How to find something online. Need info? Chances are, you can find it online—but you have to know how to search for it. Different search engines and sites provide different types of info. For example:

  - Google allows you to search the entire Web by typing in keywords associated with what you're looking for. When in doubt, simply type in a direct question, such as "what is the best way to use Google?"

  - Yahoo! Answers is a great resource for getting help from others. Simply type your specific question about, well, anything, and wait a bit. Chances are that before long, someone with the solution will see your question and provide the answer.

  - SuperPages is a great resource for finding the addresses, phone numbers, and URLs of other companies.

- How to bookmark sites in your browser so you can go back to them quickly.

- How to organize your files so you can find them easily.

PART 3

WORKING WITH PARTNERS

As you venture out into your new business, you may be considering working with a partner or maybe two. Partners can be a great way to grow your business quickly—or a one-way ticket to an unending headache that can threaten to tear your business apart. Before you decide whether to work with a partner, consider the following.

33. Think Carefully about Having Partners

Weigh the benefits of working alone against the benefits of working with partners. The following comparison provides a few of the many good and bad points about having partners. A lot of the decision really comes down to personality type and whether you can stand to share decision-making responsibilities with one or more people who have an equal say.

Pros of Having Partners

- More money put into the company to start with (or less financial burden on you)
- Multiple skill sets to tap into
- People to bounce ideas off of
- People to share the stress with
- Psychologically, someone who you can relate to

Cons of Having Partners

- More people you'll have to share profits with
- The potential for distinctly different visions of the future
- Possible resentment if one partner feels others aren't giving their fair share
- Conflicts in decision making
- Out-of-control egos

As I'll explain a bit later in this section, I've had some pretty serious problems with business partners. My first two partners were good people, but not good a fit for me when it came to running a business. After the headaches and lawsuits, you might think that I'd give up on the partnership route altogether and go it alone, but I didn't. I stuck with it, and now I have a wonderful partner, one I've worked with for years, and I can attribute much of our success to her efforts.

The last point in the "Pros" list is, in my opinion, reason enough to want to have a partner. As much as I love owning my own business, being an entrepreneur is one of the loneliest, most isolating things in the world (I'll discuss that later in the book), and having a partner is the best way to ease that isolation. Eventually, the euphoria of getting started will die down, and you'll want someone to talk to who really understands your particular brand of stress. While people outside the company can sympathize, only a partner who's in it with you can empathize.

34. Don't Sign Up with Friends or Family

When starting your company, it may seem like a good idea to form partnerships with friends or family members. Think twice before making that decision! As well as you may know them in other capacities, you'll see a different side to them and deal with them in a different way when it comes to business and money.

Stress and disagreements during work can strain your personal relationships. Sadly, business and money are often the only issues stronger than religion and politics when it comes to breaking people apart—and it may be nearly impossible to recover from personal rifts caused by business or financial stress. Ask yourself why you want to work with your friends or family. Is it really because you all share the same vision and motivation? Do you complement each other in terms of working style, strategy, and creativity? Or do you just like to hang out together and think that going into business would be kinda fun? Do it for the right reasons—or be prepared to have a lot of empty chairs at some future Thanksgiving dinner.

35. It Has to Be Equal Right from the Start

One of the more dangerous venoms to a new partnership is that of equality. If the partnership isn't equal from the outset, it could cause problems later. For example, maybe at the beginning, one partner puts in more money than the other. Maybe one partner works 70 hours a week to get the company started while the other partner tops off at 40. Maybe one partner regularly takes potential clients to expensive lunches on the company dime, while the other partner brown-bags it, meeting with potential clients in the office to avoid the heavy meal expense. These are the type of issues that can rip a company apart.

Even if the partnership is equal in terms of ownership, all it takes is for one partner, during a particularly bad argument (and there *will* be bad arguments), to say "I'm the one who put all the money into this company, so what I say goes!" or "I'm the one doing all the work, while you're rushing home every day at five o'clock!" These sentiments, which come out in the heat of the moment, often cause deep and irreparable rifts in an otherwise strong partnership. And why do they come out? Because of the initial inequality. Even if everyone said they were fine with it at the outset, it will quietly simmer below the surface, just waiting for a chance to boil over. Avoid this by keeping everything as equal as possible right from the very beginning.

36. Trust That Your Partners Mean Well

You won't agree with every decision your partners make, but keep in mind that like you, your partners have the company's best interest at heart and (hopefully) wouldn't purposely make a decision that would hurt the company. Trust them enough to move forward with decisions you may not agree with and have faith that they know what they are doing. If you can't go on faith with your partners, then you haven't selected the right people to run your business with.

This understanding should keep you from getting too heated and help you keep your temper in check. (And believe me, it can be easy to lose your temper when you think a mistake is being made.) That being said, there will certainly be times where you vehemently disagree with a decision that your partner is making, and feel like it will result in a mistake that will just be too costly to endure. In these cases, you can't just throw caution to the wind, trust in your partner, and hope for the best. Remember: It's your money, time, and future at stake, too. If you feel that strongly about a particular decision, voice your opinion. Be firm.

37. Have Similar Visions and Goals

It is vital that you and your partners share the same vision for growing the company and for the company's brand. If you have lofty dreams of building your company into a multinational conglomerate with tens of thousands of employees and your potential partners have visions of owning a small niche company that ekes out a steady annual profit, then you and your potential partners are probably not suited to starting a business together. The vision, ultimate goal, and the philosophies on how to get there need to be the same for all partners involved.

When I began my marketing agency in 1994, I did so with a good friend who I had known for pretty much my entire life. Six months later, not only was the partnership dissolved, but so was our friendship. That probably could have been avoided had I really understood his vision. While I was fine taking a risk and living without making any real money for awhile in the hopes of making a lot more later, he was more conservative. He needed a regular paycheck. When I look back on it, I believe his real vision in starting the company was to build his resume so he could get a better job later.

My next partner had a more entrepreneurial spirit and very definitely wanted to run his own company. Before we joined forces, we talked for a long time about what we each wanted, how we wanted the company to grow, the types of clients we wanted to have. There was no question that we both had the same vision—at least in theory. But in practice? Well, that was a different story. Where I was comfortable with taking risks in order to grow—something I see as a vital part of being an entrepreneur—he simply didn't have that trait. He was much more comfortable playing it safe, not making any risky bets. Ultimately, he preferred to remain small, eking out a good living without gambling at all, to risking something for the chance to achieve greater success. He talked a bigger game than he was prepared to play. The problem is, you just can't stay small *and* get larger. You can't play it safe *and* gamble. It's one or the other—there's no room for both. Five years later, the six-month legal battle for control over the company began. I ended up with the company, but only after significant losses of both time and money. And the truth is, the warning signs had been there from the beginning—if I had just bothered to look for them.

My current partner is everything she has ever claimed to be, and then some: a dedicated worker, passionate about growth, and willing to take a risk and put pride and finances on the line in order to grow. Eventually, I learned what to look for, but it took a lot of headaches to get there. You can save yourself some real aggravation—and possibly a lot of money—by making sure your goals truly align with any new partner you work with, right off the bat.

38. Divide Corporate Responsibilities

One of the dangers of having partners is that there is always the potential for one partner to take a dominant role, leaving the other partner(s) feeling left out or bitter. Dividing responsibilities can help keep that from happening. Decide early on who will shoulder what responsibilities, and then grant each partner the autonomy to do their jobs without the other partners interfering. Thanks to these divisions, things will get done more quickly and each partner will take ownership over a part of the company without feeling like anybody is stepping on his or her toes.

Division of responsibilities also touches on one of the most tenuous areas of partnerships: who gets what title. We are all pre-programmed to recognize that a certain level of authority comes with certain titles. That's not just internally, that's externally; whoever is the president will be treated a little differently—with a little more respect—by vendors, clients, bankers, etc. Even if a company is owned in equal parts by all partners (for example, two partners each owning 50 percent of the company), there can be only one president—and there is likely to be silent resentment by the partner who ends up with the lesser title. The partner with the title of vice president may say it's fine when the papers are being signed, but it could come back to haunt everyone later on.

Making sure each partner has authority over the areas of the company for which he or she is responsible is one way to lessen the blow of the lower title. Another way to even things out is to create a CEO position. Although this is not a title that you have to establish on the legal corporation papers that you fill out when you launch your company, it can still be a great equalizer in a business partnership. Allow one partner to be president (officially designated as such on the legal forms) and allow the other partner to be the CEO, even if the only place that CEO title appears is on business cards and marketing materials. It will let employees, clients, and everyone else know that the two partners are equal, and will keep everyone feeling good about their contribution.

By now, you've probably noticed that while productivity is a happy result of these efforts, this tip is really about egos, and keeping them in check as much as possible. Egos and entrepreneurs go together like gasoline and matches; if you don't handle them with care, they can be just as combustible.

39. Communication Is the Key

The key to any good partnership is communication. There will be plenty of times when you get on each other's nerves, when each of you thinks the other is making the wrong decision, and when you go home mad as hell at each other. Don't let it eat at you or build up. Talk out any differences as soon as they arise. Many of the company's key decisions will need to be made with your partners, and you can't do that if you are holding a grudge that grows stronger over time.

Instead of stewing about things, tell your partner what is bothering you as soon as possible. Get it all out in the open, even if it may hurt his or her feelings. For example, suppose you and your partner made a pitch to a potential client together and you don't like the way he handled his end of things. It may hurt his feelings to hear that, but it has to be said so that future meetings will be more successful. Open communication is the only way a company run by partners will be able to grow.

The best way to do this is to hold regularly scheduled meetings—preferably weekly—to go over everything, including budgets, finances, critiques, and general issues regarding the company, clients, and growth measures. These meetings will be easy to skip—client meetings will come up, sales calls will need to be made, and you'll be more than happy to put internal meetings off until next week. Try really hard not to skip them too often, however. Get into the habit of having these meetings religiously. If cutting into the workday is too stressful, then meet for breakfast before work and talk then, or talk over drinks at a quiet restaurant after work. However you manage it, informal updates as you pass each other in the hall aren't going to do the trick. Formal meetings are the best way to keep all parties up to date on everything that's going on within the company, make sure that everyone is on board with any important decisions, and continue feeling good about the direction the company is heading. Not keeping all partners in the loop and up to date on important issues is a sure-fire way of making someone feel left out, feel as though his or her voice isn't being heard, and eventually cause difficult personal issues that drain the business of resource and energy.

40. Give Each Other an Open and Honest Review

Regularly scheduled performance reviews give us the chance to tell our employees what they're doing right and, maybe more importantly, where we think they can improve. The idea isn't to knock anybody down or make anyone feel badly; it's to enable employees to improve their performances and become greater assets to the company. It's helpful to you as an employer, because it gives you a chance to air any frustrations or reservations you may have with an employee; and it's helpful to the employee who may not have otherwise known the area in which he or she needs to improve.

But who ever reviews the owners of the company? That's right: nobody. But that doesn't mean that you're above making mistakes and can't improve how you do your job. Partners in companies should make it a habit to review each other right along with reviewing their employees. And don't hold back. Sure, it'll be harder, because as partners you should both be equal, and chances are you've developed a friendship that makes it hard to criticize each other. You can be gentle in your criticisms, but everyone deserves a review and deserves a chance to know where they can improve themselves.

When reviewing your partners, keep these points in mind:

- Don't take the review lightly.
- Don't let it turn into a joke.
- Don't hold back for fear of hurting each other's feelings.
- Don't be spiteful.
- Don't let it turn into a fight.

Chances are, the standard employee reviews that you give aren't going to be enough. Partner reviews aren't about whether someone's shown up late or how diligent a person is. Instead, they're opportunities to discuss the quality of the business decisions each partner makes and the leadership each partner displays, and a chance to air any grievances in a healthy way. All partners want to see their company succeed—and that means accepting some healthy criticism now and then.

You'll end up spending more time in your office than anyplace else over the next few years. It's the area of space that will best represent you to your visiting clients (site checks are typical in any industry), and will be the command center where your business is done. Don't take it lightly. Put some serious thought into your office and make it a place where your business can thrive.

41. Rent an Office Outside Your Home

This is always a hot topic of debate for new entrepreneurs: Should you work from home or rent an office? There are definite pros associated with working from home: no commute time, cost savings, etc. But as far as I'm concerned, this is an easy call: No matter how small your company is, rent an office outside of your home. There's nothing wrong with having a home-based business, but the fact is most people simply don't have the self-discipline to pull it off.

Working from home takes a tremendous amount of self-discipline—more than most people possess. Working away from home, in an office, will put you in a working environment both physically and mentally, allowing you to fully concentrate on your work. Even if you can resist the refrigerator, the TV, and all the other distractions your home offers, your surroundings will play a part in your attitude and approach to working. In addition, you'll find that if you have a separate office, you'll appreciate having a home to go to as a place away from work.

At the same time, as I mentioned earlier, there are some good points associated with working from home. Although I'm a strict advocate of renting external office space, one particularly attractive benefit of the home office is the tax advantage. There are all sorts of deductions you can take with a home office that will make April a much happier month. I'm not a CPA, so I won't go into details here; I recommend talking it over with your accountant before making any firm decisions.

42. Look Into Renting an Office Suite

No matter where you want to start your business, chances are you can find an office suite to rent somewhere nearby. An office suite is a building that rents small offices to small companies that want a more official corporate presence and more services than they could get from working at home.

Some of the benefits of renting an office suite include the following:

- Office suites are usually pretty inexpensive and shouldn't be cost-prohibitive, even for very small start-ups.
- Most office suites provide a bank of receptionists that will answer your phones using your company's name.
- Typically, you can pay a little extra (usually an hourly fee) for secretarial services.
- Most office suites give you access to conference rooms that you can use for client meetings.
- Most have services that help you send outgoing mail and will sort incoming mail for you as well.

The biggest benefit, however, is that renting an office suite gives you the ability to work away from your home, and to be in a building with many other small startup companies. You'll end up making friends and, depending on the type of business you're in, you may also end up getting a few new clients. When I rented my first office suite, I got all this and more: I made a few good friends (with whom I still keep in touch); I dated one of the secretaries for awhile; I grabbed a few early clients, one of which I still work with today (over 15 years later); and, best of all, met Deirdre Breakenridge, who worked two offices down from me, and who years later would become by business partner (and one of the biggest forces behind our success as a company).

43. Keep Your Home Office Apart from Your Home

If you do decide to run the company out of your home instead of renting outside office space, make sure you put it somewhere out of the way, and set it up to resemble a traditional office as best as you can. Let everyone else in the house—especially kids—know that your office is off limits. If possible, choose a room in the house that has its own entrance so you don't have to traipse clients through the entire house to get to your office.

Most importantly is the need to put yourself in the right mindset for working. No matter how disciplined you are, the mindset changes as soon as you walk into a space that's specifically designated for work. Mentally, you need this space to fully focus on making smart corporate decisions. Building a company takes a lot of concentration. If you've ever played a sport for a high-school or college team, then you know the importance of being "in the zone"—the state of mind that enables you to get ready to play with everything you've got and win. You also know that you get in the zone in the locker room or on the field—not in your living room. Your company is the same way. You're simply not going to be in the zone with Maury Povich on TV and all the comforts of home surrounding you. You need to set aside a room that you can walk into and know immediately, "This is where I come to do my work." Having the right frame of mind is important to making the smart decisions you'll need to make to build your company.

44. Make Your Office Comfortable for Clients

Whether your office is in your home or in an office building, make sure it is accommodating to the clients who will inevitably come visit you. (You always want to have meetings at your place for a home-court advantage.) Get a few really comfortable chairs or a couch for visiting clients to sit on and small incidentals for them to enjoy, like really good, high-quality coffee. It doesn't hurt to provide a water cooler and soft drinks, either. It will be worth the expense.

45. Keep Your Office Worthy of Your Title

How your office looks will go a long way in negotiations and meetings. Remember—and it'll be tough to forget, given how many times I mention it in this book—that perception and presentation are everything in client relations.

Your personal office should look like the office of, well, a company president or CEO. Give the office a good paint job and get nice furniture so that when an employee or a client walks in for a meeting, the first impression they get is that you are a person of accomplishment.

In addition, decorate the office in a way that shows off and markets your company. If you're a small architectural firm, hang framed pictures of some of the structures you've built. Meaningful touches like this do a lot more to market your company than photographs of your family. If nothing else, ditch those horrible "Successories" posters; they're really annoying.

46. Invest in a Security System for the Office

If you're using an expensive computer system or other high-tech equipment, think seriously about investing in a security system that uses motion detectors, alarms, or other methods to protect your workspace. Insurance policies might cover the cost of the computer in the event it's stolen, but you won't be able to recoup the value of the files—yours and your clients—stored inside the computer. The greatest loss will come from the amount of time you are out of commission because your equipment is gone. Plus, in most cases, your insurance costs will be lower if you have a security system installed.

PART 5

GETTING A GRIP ON FINANCES

One of the most important—and possibly the most frightening and misunderstood—parts of starting a new business is understanding the finances. Unfortunately, there's a bit more to it than simply "Close the deal, do the work, invoice, get paid, repeat the process." Make sure you have a firm grip on all money issues before diving in and finding yourself in deeper waters than you can handle.

47. You'll Need Some of Your Own Money to Start

Every company—even small service companies that you can run from your home—has some startup expenses. Granted, service companies won't cost you the big-time dollars associated with manufacturing, inventory, and shipping, but there are smaller costs you need to be aware of. Here's a list of just a few that immediately come to mind:

- You'll need to pay a filing fee to get the company officially registered, plus a legal fee if you have a lawyer do it (which I recommend).

- Depending on your bank and the type of business account you open, you may be required to keep a certain amount (my bank requires $500) in the account at all times. Plus, there are fees for ordering checks.

- There are phone lines and business phones to consider (business phones usually have different features than standard home phones). Alternatively, if you choose to go the cell-phone route, there are those bills to account for.

- You're going to need a fax machine, a computer, software, a printer, and more, as detailed earlier in this book.

- Physical file cabinets, folders, a dry-erase board, and other office supplies are going to cost money.

- Don't forget the expense of having your logo designed, or at the very least getting your business cards printed.

- You'll need a Web site, and unless you're building a Web development company, that's going to cost you something, as will hosting fees.

- You're going to have to drive to clients, events, meetings, and other places associated with your business, which means paying for gas and tolls.

- If you meet potential clients for lunch or dinner, guess who's paying for that... you.

- If you have an opportunity to do business with a potential client on the other side of the country, you're going to need to lay out the money for a plane ticket, transportation to and from the airport, food, and a hotel.

I could go on, but I'm sure you get the idea. This money has to come from somewhere, and that somewhere is your pocket. And don't simply sweep costs under the rug by making excuses like "Well, I need to get a new computer anyway," or "If I had taken a job, I may have had to drive even further, costing me even more in gas and tolls." It doesn't work like that. Quite frankly, for tax reasons, you don't want it to work like that—there are tax benefits that come with accumulating business-related expenses. But one way or the other, all these items and more need to be paid for. You'll want to have this money up front before starting your company. To be safe, make sure you have enough to get you through the first six months at the very least. Longer is better, but six months is a bare minimum.

48. Don't Count on Clients to Fund the Startup Phase of Business

Many entrepreneurs, passionate and ready to believe their own hype, go into business thinking that it's all a very simple process:

1. Open up shop.
2. Get a new client.
3. Complete a project.
4. Get paid.
5. Repeat.

I hate to be the one to break it to you, but it doesn't work that way. Not even close, actually. It's just not realistic to count on revenue from client projects to fund you in the early days. Here's a slightly more realistic order of events:

1. You open your company.
2. You work like crazy to find your first client.
3. The client takes longer than you expect to decide whether to use your services.
4. After weeks or even months of putting it off, the client finally decides to move forward.
5. If they're a smaller company, you can probably get a deposit—maybe 50 percent, but more likely 33 percent. That will help cover some of the expenses you've incurred during the time the client made you wait, plus some of the money you'll need to spend to do the job for the client.
6. If the terms for the balance due are net 30 days from completion, then you might get lucky and you might get paid on time. Chances are, though, that the payment will come late and you'll have to chase the client for the money they owe you, costing you additional time and energy that could be put to better use in new sales or completing projects for other clients.
7. If the terms for the balance due are payment upon completion of the project but the client isn't quite ready to pay, then they'll do everything in their power to delay the completion of the project, making you run in unnecessary circles. Maybe they'll be slow to give feedback or make a series of unnecessary changes. Any of these situations will be costly to you because not only does it require more work on your part, but it's more time that you'll go without having the money they owe you.

In short, while you might budget for, say, netting $10,000 within two months, the reality could end up being $7,000 after more than four or five months. That's painful for any small company to endure. If you're counting on that revenue to keep you afloat, it could be more than painful; it could be downright deadly.

49. Consider Using a Smaller Bank

You'll need to open a bank account for your company that's separate from your personal bank account. My suggestion: Use a smaller, local bank that will take genuine interest in your company and future. Larger banks, while they may be more accessible because they have more branches in more locations, are also bound by their own internal rulebook and are more likely to treat your company like a number. Smaller banks, on the other hand, will be more lenient and willing to work with you, and more likely to take risks on your behalf as your relationship with them progresses.

My own agency has used the same bank for over a decade. They're a smaller community bank, about 30 minutes away, and although it's somewhat inconvenient (especially compared to the Citibank right across the street from us), I don't see us ever taking our account elsewhere. That's because they treat us like real people. They've gotten to know my partner and me, and they've come to trust us. They've also come to save us when we needed them, such as when all our clients are suddenly super late paying very large bills and we have to make payroll; they'll cover it on our word that the money is coming. It doesn't happen often, but when it does, it's good to know that we have a bank we can rely on. Larger banks simply can't—and don't—do that sort of thing. When you're running a small company, you'll need all the advantages you can get—and finding a bank that will really help you grow is a good step in the right direction.

50. Don't Take Funds from Friends or Family

People who write business books love to write the same thing: If you need money to fund your business, look to family and friends. In truth, friends and family should be your final resort. The last thing you're going to want to do is constantly explain to your family how your business is going so they know when they'll get their money back. Even if they say "Don't worry about it, there's no rush" or assure you that they don't care if it gets paid back at all, you'll have some pretty uncomfortable Thanksgiving dinners when you show pictures of your recent vacation to Hawaii to the uncle who is still waiting for you to pay back the start-up money he lent you. Family and friends are great to have in your life for emotional support; financial support, though, is another matter entirely.

51. Seeking Venture Capital? Good Luck!

If you were awake at all during the mid to late 1990s, you're undoubtedly familiar with the term "venture capitalist," which was used repeatedly in conjunction with the many (and often ridiculous) Web startups launched at the start of the dot-com boom. A venture capitalist is an individual or company that provides the funding (usually in the millions of dollars) for a small company to get off the ground.

The chances of your small, risky business being funded by a venture capitalist are so low, however, that you're probably better off spending your time playing one of those ridiculous national lotteries. Depending on which source you want to rely on, venture capitalists fund anywhere from .01 to 2 percent of the all companies that send them proposals. Not great odds.

If you want to attempt the venture capitalist route, have a really well thought-out business plan ready for them to analyze and dissect, including three- to five-year financial projections. You should also be prepared for the decision-making process to take a long while—there are typically four or five rounds of meetings and analysis before decisions start being made. Don't forget: Venture capitalists have a finite amount of money to invest and piles upon piles of business opportunities to choose from, so you'll have to really know your market and be able to sell them on your potential.

Be warned that if you do end up working with a venture capitalist, chances are they're not just going to be a silent partner. They'll expect a significant percentage of your corporate stock and will likely be involved in (or at least scrutinize) many of the decisions you'll make about the growth of your company.

52. Different Loans Have Different Purposes

There are a few types of loans available for new-business owners:

- Friends and family are often resources for finances—although as I mentioned earlier, this can be dangerous and needs to be carefully considered. If you do accept financing from friends or family members, don't do it on a hand-shake. Have a formal contract drawn up for all parties.

- An asset-secured bank loan provides you with a specific amount of money you can use to buy assets, build inventory, or fill other needs. These loans are typically payable on a monthly basis over a pre-established amount of time and backed by assets such as your home, government bonds, etc.

- A credit line is a set amount of money that you can tap into during times when cash flow is low, and is payable at your convenience when cash flow is high again. This is helpful when, for example, you have to make payroll but you're short on cash.

- Credit cards are a popular means for people to fund their new business ventures. They provide instant cash as you need it, with far less paperwork than you'd have to fill out if you went to a bank. But beware: Interest rates can be high. And while it might be tempting to just pay the minimum payment each month, before you know it, your interest payments will be higher than your initial balance.

While you're not going to want to take on too much debt, borrowing money to fund some aspect of your business is more than likely just a matter of time. Whether it's to make purchases to get the company up and running, expedite growth, buy necessary supplies to complete an upcoming client project, or make next week's payroll, borrowing money is typically a foregone conclusion in the life of the entrepreneur. Understand the different loan options available to you so you can make the best choice based on the situation at hand at the most affordable rates possible.

53. Don't Wait Until the Last Minute

The worst time to approach a banker is the day you realize you're short on cash. Apply for a loan well before you really need it. The loan process can be long, and there's no guarantee that the outcome will be in your favor. Like anything else, getting a loan from a bank is about building relationships. The sooner you start one with your banker, the better off you'll be. This is particularly true when it comes to establishing a line of credit, which makes money available to you in case of emergency. Chances are greater that you'll be approved for the line when you're not already in an emergency situation.

54. Keep Accurate Records of All Bank and Loan Transactions

Entrepreneurs are known for their creativity. By and large, however, they are not known for being organized or particularly good with keeping up with their books. Ideally, you'll have a bookkeeper to handle anything that has to do with day-to-day finances, but it's more likely that you'll be handling these issues yourself at the beginning. Don't be lazy about it. Keeping accurate records of all banking transactions as well as all payables and receivables will be necessary to get any type of cooperation from a bank regarding a loan. Your best bet is to invest in QuickBooks, one of the more widely used bookkeeping software products on the market. It will help you keep everything in line and make tracking your finances a little easier. That way, when you need to show your records to your bank, everything will be ready for you.

55. Bankers Look for Specific Information

If you seek loan assistance from a bank, you'll need to be prepared to show them all the things they're going to ask for and be ready to answer all the questions they're sure to pose. These include the following:

■ A list of your accountants and what systems of accounting they use.

- Biographies of management (that's you and any partners/key employees), written to convince them that you have experience in the industry or relevant experience outside it. Be able to demonstrate management experience to prove that you will make good decisions for your company in the future.
- Proof that your company is in a growth industry or at least not in a shrinking one. If you're planning to open a spa for pet rocks, you might not find a bank to lend you money.
- An overview of the personnel structure in place, including accountants, lawyers, managers, employees, and vendors who will take care of various aspects of the business.
- Cash-flow projections and the potential for profitability from that cash flow.

56. Between a Rock and a Hard Place? Sell Your Receivables

This is not a tip I would suggest you dive into on a regular basis, but in a crunch it can come in handy. Unfortunately, not many banks will accept accounts receivable as collateral against a loan. But there are companies that will purchase your account receivables and supply you with immediate cash. In a severe pinch, these types of arrangements can be a life saver—and they're at least a little more legit and a little less scary than one you'll make with a back alley loan shark who'll have your thumbs broken if you don't pay the loan back in time.

If you choose to work with one of these companies (you can find one by looking them up online), know in advance that it will cost you. Companies that purchase receivables can charge 10 percent or even higher. Usually, the percentage charged is based on a number of factors, including the following

- The credit rating of you and your company
- The credit rating of the client from whom you are awaiting payment
- The amount in question
- How immediately you need the funds

In the end, it will cost you a lot to engage in this kind of financial practice. If the fee is 20 percent, for example, on a receivable of $20,000, then you're giving up $4,000. That's a steep price to pay. But if you're in a serious bind and need cash fast, it's good to know that this type of option is available.

57. The SBA Can Be Tough, but Useful

People are often confused by what the Small Business Administration (SBA) really is and does. The SBA is a U.S. government agency that does not typically offer loans directly to small businesses. Instead, you apply for your loan through your bank, with the SBA guaranteeing most of the loan. This significantly reduces the bank's risk, increasing your chances of being approved for your loan.

The SBA has multiple programs for business owners to choose from depending on need and other factors and can include small business training and counseling if desired.

There are two big drawbacks associated with SBA loans:

■ They require a lot of collateral on your part.

■ The amount of paperwork can be quite daunting.

On the flip side, the SBA gives you more time to repay loans and usually offers better interest rates than a bank. Also, even though they do ask for more collateral than you might expect, they will often accept collateral such as valuable art, antiques, rare coins, or jewelry and other such items, which a bank generally won't accept.

58. It's All About the Personal Assets

The biggest key to obtaining bank loans is to have collateral. Banks lend money on the expectation that the loan will be paid back, with interest. But that expectation isn't based on the fact that the nice banker thinks you have an honest face and seem like a swell sort of person. No, the bank is going to want something of value to back the loan—something they can keep if you fail to repay it. Different banks accept different things as collateral; some (very, very few) even accept receivables as collateral against a loan. Most, however, are happy with one thing: real estate.

Owning your own home can be an important part of growing a business. Aside from the tax benefits you can receive, your home will make excellent collateral for a bank loan (assuming you have a decent amount of equity in your home at the time you require your business loan). There are also opportunities, in a financial crunch, to take second mortgages on your home and to pull equity out of your home in situations where you're in dire need of cash. These all do take some time, so if you want to take these routes, don't wait until the last minute.

Remember, though, that using your home as collateral is a dangerous game. Although I've discussed the need for entrepreneurs to take risks and gamble to achieve success, betting your home is not something you can be cavalier about. Losing your home is serious business, and when you put it down as collateral, it becomes a very real possibility if things in your company don't go in the right direction.

59. Hire a Smart Financial Advisor

As the owner of your company, your main job will be to manage, sell, and innovate. Don't feel inadequate if you're not good with handling money; it's a talent that many people simply don't have. It shouldn't keep you from pursuing your dreams of building a viable company.

Your best bet is to hire a financial advisor who can help you manage your money. I don't mean someone who comes in once a year to do your taxes; I'm talking about an individual who can really get know you and your company to help you make sound, customized investment decisions that will enable you to reach your goals. More than once in my career, I wanted to go pie-eyed into an investment opportunity that my financial planner soberly told me I simply couldn't afford. I'm not ashamed to tell you that in hindsight, the times that I refused to listen—well, let's just say I wish I had.

You should think of your financial planner as part of your overall planning and growth team, helping to move the company forward on a regular basis. He or she should help you prepare and balance all your books, generate forecasts and budgets for upcoming quarters, and make suggestions on how to reinvest profits, forge relationships with banks, help secure lines of credit, and break down revenue and expenditures so that you know what products/services are selling better than others and how your money is being spent. And, as I referenced earlier, he or she should also be the voice of reason when you want to spend more money than your budget will allow.

When selecting an advisor, make sure you choose one with the same investment mindset as yourself. If you're the careful, cautious type, don't select a financial advisor who is too aggressive in his strategies. Conversely, if you're looking to take some risks and want to invest more aggressively, don't work with someone who is too conservative. Every investment choice you make ultimately needs to improve your personal wealth and security and advance your company in one way or another, so make sure you're not at odds with the advisor you choose.

Finally, no matter how much you feel like you trust the financial advisor you're working with, and no matter how much you hate dealing with the money yourself, don't fully trust anybody. Make sure that every dollar is accounted for and that you okay every investment. All it takes is one dishonest individual take advantage of someone else's trusting nature for everything you've worked for to completely fall apart.

60. Don't Go Nuts with Spending

Don't overpay for anything. Sometimes, especially during the beginning stages of growing your company, or just after you make a large sale, your excitement will lead you to spend more on items than you have to or buy things you don't really need. Throwing money around and buying expensive things is a fairly typical entrepreneurial trait; it's hard to feel like a CEO when you're trying to save a few nickels on basic purchases. But when you're just starting your company, you've got to try to save money where you can. Wasteful spending adds up!

Don't overuse your accountant or lawyer (they charge you by the hour), rush out and by the $3,000 oak desk you've had your eye on, or stock up on 10,000 reams of paper just because you like to feel important when you're cruising the aisles at Office Depot. Buy just what you need, look for less expensive—but still attractive—furniture, and seek out any other avenue you can find to keep your expenses down until the company is in a good position for to spend available funds a bit more freely.

61. Sticker Prices Don't Always Apply

Some people love to negotiate; there's a certain thrill that comes with talking down a price, and securing a product or service at a much lower cost. For other people, however, negotiating prices causes a nauseating feeling in the pit of their stomach, and they quickly accept any price quoted just to avoid the confrontation. If the latter description applies to you, you may want to rethink opening your own company. Not only will you need good negotiation skills to secure the highest prices for what you are selling, but it will be just as important to negotiate down to get the lowest prices for what you are buying.

Most items outside of supermarkets and lower-priced retail stores are negotiable. Car dealers are known for their willingness to negotiate on price. The prices of high-end electronics, including those bought at major-name retailers like Best Buy, are typically negotiable as well.

There are two basic rules of thumb when it comes to what can and can't be negotiated:

- The higher the price of an item, the more likely it is you can wheel and deal a bit. Going back to Best Buy, for example, a large-screen plasma TV with a ticket price of $1,500 can absolutely be negotiated down in price, while season three of *The Office* on DVD for $29.95 is non-negotiable.

- Products and services provided by small, non-chain, and B2B providers usually have some wiggle room. Printers, interior decorators, accountants, marketing agencies—all of these types of companies understand that their prices will likely be negotiated downward. In fact, they'll often jack up their prices to begin with due to the expectation that the final sale will be lower.

The final prices that you secure will ultimately play a big role in how you price your own products and services, the profit margin you receive, and whether your company can be competitive in your marketplace. So don't be afraid to be tough in your negotiations. Obviously, your vendors will need to make a profit as well, but walk away if you don't feel like you're getting the best deal you can get. Let them chase you rather than the other way around; that way, you can negotiate from a position of power. Get prices from multiple vendors for anything that you need to buy; this will give you an idea of what a fair price actually is. It will also put your vendors on the defense, knowing they're in competition for your business. Finally, if you can't make a deal work, find another vendor. Don't just settle or be afraid to negotiate. Bringing down your costs is a necessity to growing your business.

62. Make Great Deals with Smaller Companies

As your business grows, there will be a lot of people and companies wanting to sell you stuff. You should be the one who sets the tone for any business you do together. Whenever you negotiate with a vendor—especially a small vendor that is hungry for work—you have the upper hand. You're the one signing the checks, after all. Tell smaller companies that you'll be willing to give them a shot, but require that they either charge you a lower fee or even work for free on an initial project so you can evaluate their quality. The benefit to them, of course, is the promise that you may use them for larger, more profitable projects later on.

That being said, don't go overboard leveraging your dominant position. Your vendors need to be happy with the deal, too, or you won't get their best work from them. And remember: Eventually, you and your company will be someone else's vendor. Make beneficial deals for yourself, but don't go so far overboard that you're ultimately seen as being unfair and impossible to deal with.

63. Calculate the Real Bottom Line

You need to figure out what your true net profit (TNP) is on each project you work on. If you don't figure out the true net profit, you could be budgeting and spending more money than you actually have.

The equation for finding your true net profit isn't too difficult:

gross sales − vendor fees − total cost of project (total employee cost [individual hourly salaries of employees working on a given account × the number of hours worked on said account]) + (total hard recurring cost [the number of hours worked by all employees on said account × hard recurring costs per employee per hour]) = TNP

First, you need to figure out your hard recurring costs—rent, average telephone bills, utilities, etc.—and what those costs equate to per employee per hour. Assume for the sake of example that number is $30—in other words, it costs you $30 per hour per employee just to stay in business. Next, let's assume your company is a graphic-design shop with two employees: John and Mary. Both are designers, assigned to work on the XYZ account, which is billed out to XYZ Corp. at $125 per hour. John's hourly salary is roughly $22 per hour, and Mary's is $27.50 per hour. John and Mary spend 20 hours each working on the account, for a total of 40 hours. Vendor fees for the XYZ account are $1,000, for printing costs. So to figure out the true net profit for this account, we'd plug the numbers into the equation as follows:

$125/hour × 40 hours worked	= $5,000 gross sales
Minus vendor costs	= $1,000
NET AFTER VENDOR	= $4,000
Mary: $27.50/hour × 20 hours	= $550
Plus John: John: $22/hour × 20 hours	= $440
TOTAL EMPLOYEE COST	= $990
40 hours worked × $30	= $1,200
Plus total employee cost	= $990
TOTAL COST OF PROJECT	= $2,190
Net after vendor revenue	= $4,000
Minus total cost of project	= $2,190
TRUE NET PROFIT	**= $1,810**

Scary, isn't it? When you do the math, you really don't make as much on a $5,000 sale as you think you do. Too often, small companies base buying decisions on the Net After Vendor (NAV) profit—that is, gross sales − vendor costs—and never figure out why they're always losing money.

For the first few years of running my own company, I used a very basic method of budgeting and determining profits. If I charged a client $10,000 for a project and it cost me $5,000 in materials, then my profit was $5,000. Then I would use that $5,000 figure to set my budgets. In other words, I would use that $5,000 profit to make $5,000 in purchases, either on my credit cards or through new leases or using cash outright. Pretty simple, right? Over time, though, I constantly lost money, and I could never figure out why. It turned out that ongoing costs like rent, utilities, and salaries that weren't associated with a particular job never got figured into any equation but continued to add up all the same. Once I began to figure them into my profit/loss projections, not only was I able to set my prices more wisely, I was able to budget more realistically so that I could actually *afford* my purchases.

64. Concentrate on Work by Farming Out Personal Chores

Through the years, I've discussed this rule with many people—most of whom seem to conclude that this is simply a clever way to justify why I don't bother to clean my home or engage in other domestic chores. And while it's true that I don't particularly like to clean, this rule is actually one that I firmly believe in—and it makes total sense, considering most entrepreneurs' work ethic.

The basic philosophy goes something like this: As a business owner, you don't live a 9-to-5 existence. Your working hours are from the time you wake up in the morning to the time you go to bed at night. During regular working hours, you'll be busy trying to run the company, complete projects, and find new clients. During the rest of the day, you'll be thinking about your business—developing new ideas, putting together new lists of potential contacts. It never really ends. The end goal, of course, is to grow your business, make back your investment, and generate a sizable profit. Every hour you work is an hour put toward reaching that goal. Conversely, every hour you *don't* work is an hour you *don't* put toward reaching that goal. Your time is valuable, so don't waste it on chores that have less financial value.

For example, let's look at housecleaning. Suppose it would cost $100 to hire a housekeeper to come in and clean your home. Now let's say that your own time is worth $50 per hour (what you would charge a client for an hour of service). If it takes you four hours to clean your home—time you *could* be putting into your business—you're essentially spending $200 to have the place cleaned ($50 per hour × four hours), and probably not clean it all that well. That's twice as much as you'd spend hiring someone to do it for you. In essence, by hiring someone, you're saving $100.

The same rule goes for mowing the lawn and similar chores. It's hard to grasp, because hiring someone to do non–work-related chores for you is an expense—it's cash out of your pocket—where doing it yourself means keeping your cash. But if you manage your time properly (in other words, if you use the time you're saving to work on your company and move the business forward), then spending the cash and investing more time into entrepreneurial endeavors is great trade-off in the long run.

65. You Need to Invest in Order to Grow

Money, especially when it's scarce, can be tough to part with. If your idea of saving money is to put used paper in the fax machine instead of spending $3 on a new ream, I gotta be honest with you: Growth is not in your future. Business growth demands investing in the right areas, not cutting corners. For example, hiring a salesperson who is right out college will save you a lot of money—$30,000 per year in salary rather than $80,000 or more for someone with experience and connections. But who's more likely to bring in higher revenue over the long haul?

The point is, ultra-conservatism and aggressive business growth don't go together. Yes, you'll need to watch your funds and spend money wisely, but don't risk your future by failing to allocate the right amount of money where it's needed. Think long-term, and make the right investments.

66. Set Your Budgets Way in Advance

Spending money haphazardly rarely has any real benefit. Instead, establish budgets for your company based on a percentage of true net revenue. Decide early on to spend a certain percentage of your true net revenue on marketing and advertising, another percentage on entertaining clients, a set percentage on basic office needs, etc. That way, you won't end up spending more than what you have—and if you do need more in one area, you'll know what other area needs to suffer because of it.

Keep a close eye on what your company is really gaining from its expenses. For example, suppose you set a budget of $2,000 per month on entertaining clients and $500 per month on sending direct e-mail solicitations. If both efforts are bringing in 10 new customers per week, then you might want to think about redirecting your entertainment budget. Even though you were able to gain some additional clients through expensive dinners and drinks, the cost of gaining each of those clients was far greater than the per-client cost of the direct e-mail efforts. By keeping track of things like that, you can better plan for the future.

67. You'll Need Cash to Facilitate Large Accounts

Be prepared for new accounts to cost you money before you can earn a profit from them. For example, say that your company lands a huge account with Nike. Total gross revenue of the account is well over a million dollars, with a good net profit built in. But because of the size of the project, you're going to need to hire more people and order far more supplies than you usually keep in stock. And with a company that large, you've got virtually no shot of getting a deposit; the client's accounting system doesn't work like that, and you'll look weak if you ask for it. The best you can hope for is to be paid a portion of the account 30 days from the date they receive the invoice (although 45 days may be more like it). The ramp up for the project is going to cost you some pretty big bucks, so be prepared to find a way to get the project off the ground without relying on money from the client in the early stages.

68. Don't Forget to Charge Sales and Use Tax

A long time ago, a few years after opening my company, we ran into some serious problems because we didn't understand that we needed to collect tax on services as well as on products. Eventually, the government came looking for their money—and guess who's pocket that came out of?

Different states have different laws regarding sales and use tax. Make sure you understand how these laws work in your state and what tax rate you need to charge. Basically, it's up to you to collect these taxes from your clients, retain the funds, and then pass them on to the government. It will be important for you to understand what, exactly, is supposed to be taxed.

Some companies may be able to provide you with paperwork showing you that they are exempt from paying these taxes. Make sure you collect these and keep good records of them. For everyone else, make sure you add the taxes to each invoice. If you don't, it will be very hard to go back to your client and ask them to pay the neglected amount after the fact. If you forgot to invoice it, it can potentially be damaging to the relationship to request the taxes later. Finally, don't forget to put the collected taxes aside. You'll end up in a bad financial situation if you spend the taxes you've collected on your own company and have nothing left when it's time to turn the taxes over to the government.

69. Consider Leasing Rather Than Buying Equipment

Equipment costs can be a major expense for a small company. If you're cash-poor (as most startups are), it can be tough to find the capital necessary to buy the equipment you need to run your business. Rather than purchasing equipment, consider leasing it instead. Leasing equipment can give you a number of advantages, including the following:

- Leasing will free up the cash you would need to purchase your equipment, leaving you free to use it for payroll or other expenses.

- If you borrow money from a bank to make your equipment purchase, the loan is a debt, and its repayment is simply facilitating that debt. However, payments on a lease are considered an expense, which will improve your financial outlook and help you at tax time.

- When you purchase equipment, it's depreciated over several years. But the monthly expenses of leasing equipment are all deducted in the current year.

- As I mentioned earlier, getting a bank loan isn't always easy. You'll need to provide collateral and engage in a significant amount of paperwork to qualify for your loan. Companies that lease equipment, on the other hand, won't likely look too far beyond your credit history for the past year or so. If your credit is good enough, you may even get your equipment without having to put any money down.

- When you purchase your equipment, you'll end up having to pay extra over its life span each time you need to have it serviced or fixed. This can add up. With a lease, however, maintenance is usually part of the deal; you won't have to pay extra each time the equipment runs down or needs repair.

- Technology changes quickly; equipment is often obsolete before you know it. When you purchase equipment, you're stuck with it until you're financially able to buy new equipment. That means if new innovations come out shortly after you've made your purchase, you'll end up being behind your competitors. And by the time you're ready to upgrade, the equipment you own may not have any resale value. With a lease, however, you can upgrade more rapidly, and not be in fear of falling behind the times.

70. Retain a Payroll Company for Your Employees

As soon as you get more than five employees, hire a payroll company. Unfortunately, payroll involves more than simply writing a check. There are all sorts of other payments that need to be processed, such as payroll taxes; Social Security withholdings; worker's-comp insurance, health-care and 401(k) payments (if you offer those benefits); local, state, and federal tax withholdings; and more. This makes payroll a supreme headache and potentially a financial nightmare. Your best bet is to let someone else do it—someone who'll get it done right and allow you to concentrate on running your business. Chances are, your accounting firm or financial planner can provide these services. If not, look into using a company such as Ceridian (my personal preference) or ADP to manage your payroll.

71. Payroll Is a Big Expense; There Are Ways to Ease the Pain

If you have employees, your biggest ongoing expense will be payroll. It's not just the money that's owed to your employees for their salary; there are tax expenses that need to be paid to the government within a short period of time after paychecks are deposited. Payroll taxes, Social Security, workman's comp insurance—all of these are fees that go along with payroll and can add up quickly.

Of course, the hardest part about this is having the cash on hand. Employees usually get paid every two weeks, so it ends up being a lot of money out of the company's bank account on a regular basis. No matter what, this is going to be painful—but there are ways to ease the pain if you're running low on cash:

- As I mentioned earlier, establish a credit line with a bank. Credit lines are used for short-term loans in case there's a cash crunch.

- Don't do direct deposit; pay your employees by check instead.

- Ask employees to deposit their checks rather than cash them. This will allow a few more days to pass before the money leaves your account—that's a few more days to collect more cash from customers who owe you money.

- Pay employees on a Friday and hand out checks after 3:00 p.m. If you hand checks out in the morning, employees can deposit them during lunch. Handing checks out later in the day will keep them from depositing them immediately; and when it comes to banks, doing anything after 3:00 p.m. is pretty much the equivalent of doing it the following business day. So after 3:00 p.m. on Friday is the same as Monday morning.

■ If you have a good relationship with a smaller, local bank, call them and explain your situation. There's a chance you might convince them to cover payroll until you get more money in from clients.

■ In a severe crunch, tell your employees that you need to push payroll back a day or two. They won't like it, but sometimes it has to be done—and it's better than having to lay someone off.

One last thing to remember when considering how to deal with payroll: If you pay your employees every two weeks, you'll be paying them twice each month, with two exceptions. Two months every year, you'll have to deal with three payrolls. Those will be expensive months. Look at a calendar and figure out when those months are based on your pay schedule and prepare for them in advance.

72. Always Have a Working Credit Card

Okay, so there we were in a restaurant in Chicago: me, one of my employees, and two of our clients from one of our largest accounts. We went through about three bottles of wine, a menu full of appetizers, all of our main courses, and a tray of desserts. Eventually, the check came, totaling somewhere around $700. No biggie; I took out my debit card and handed it to the waitress. Ten minutes later, she returned, saying that my card had been declined. (Apparently, my bank's computers were down.) Few things have ever been more embarrassing.

Make sure you have a credit card on you at all times that is nowhere near being maxed out. Taking a client to lunch only to find out that your credit card has been rejected is incredibly damaging, and most of us look silly trying to fumble around for cash to pay the bill. And don't rely on a bank debit card, even if it has a MasterCard or Visa logo on it. For some reason, sometimes those cards are rejected even if you have plenty of money in your account.

73. Don't Let Your Clients Know About Any Financial Problems

Clients want to work with companies that are financially sound—that they know will be around next week. This is especially true if they are contemplating hiring your company to complete a large project that will take an extended period of time. The fear, of course, is that they'll get a project started only to find halfway into it that your company is out of business.

No matter how comfortable you feel with a client and no matter how many projects you've done for them, don't let them know you're having financial problems or even a temporary cash crunch. That doesn't just mean refraining from coming right out and discussing it directly, it also means not giving them subtle hints that will tip them off to any problems. For example, if you typically work on a net-30 basis and suddenly ask for a deposit, if you begin nickel and diming small items when you've never done so in the past, or if you ask for existing invoices to be expedited, these can all be hints that set off a client's radar, causing them to ask questions. Tip them off too much or give them reason for serious concern, and they may push projects back until they feel more comfortable—or worse, they might cancel the project altogether, finding another, more financially sound vendor to work with.

As hard as it is, do your best to put a smile on your face during client interactions and keep any financial problems to yourself. The best way out of a cash crunch is to increase your sales. That won't be an option if you scare clients off.

74. Seven Years Can Last a Lifetime

Earlier, I discussed the different types of businesses you can start and how some of them can limit your personal liability. While that's legally true, in the everyday practice of doing business, there aren't many organizations that are going to extend credit to your company without wanting personal guarantees from you as well—at least during the early years, before your company is established and has a positive credit history.

That means it's imperative that you keep your personal credit rating in good standing. Having a low credit score or a credit report with too many damaging items on it can prevent you from getting necessary credit and favorable payment terms from vendors you work with, in turn forcing you to come up with hefty up-front deposits for products and services you need. Over time, as your company pays its bills in a timely fashion, its credit will become established; eventually, your personal guarantees won't be needed any longer.

If you do fall behind, understand that your credit will be damaged—and nothing will fix that except time. Bad marks on a credit report take seven years to go away—which can be a long time to wait to get favorable rates and payment terms.

75. Stay in Touch with Creditors

People tend to be cowards, shying away from confrontation or potentially uncomfortable situations. It's easy enough to be invisible and avoid issues simply by not answering the phone when creditors call and ignoring mail demanding payment on overdue bills. But you can't stay invisible for very long; eventually, creditors will catch up to you—and when they do, it'll likely get really ugly, really fast.

The best strategy is to not let it get to that point to begin with. The truth is, there is one thing most companies want more than money: communication. Most—not all, but most—will understand if you're going through a tight period without a lot of cash and will be willing to work with you. Some may let you skip a payment and have some time to catch up; others may work with you to set up a payment plan that breaks up larger bills into smaller ones that you can more easily afford. But you need to stay in touch with them, and you need to be honest. Explain that the situation you're experiencing is temporary, tell them why it happened (maybe your customers are late paying you), tell them how you're going to regain stability, and reassure them that you want to work with them to get them paid.

Yours won't be the first company to run into a cash-flow problem; most creditors and vendors to whom you owe money will know this, and most will have dealt with this problem before. But chances are they're more used to having companies that owe them money giving them the run-around or avoiding them altogether. Stay in touch, communicate, and work with them, and you'll likely get through rough patches a lot more smoothly.

76. Create a List of Who Gets Paid First

At some point, unless you are very well funded from the outset, you're going to run into a cash crunch and will need to decide who gets paid and who doesn't. Make a list of all of your creditors and prioritize them in the following order:

1. Pay off any company that has the ability to turn off something important, such as telephones or Internet services. If you need a service to survive, then keep those companies paid.

2. Although this is item #2 on the list, you should understand it's a very close second: Pay the government any money you owe. Holding off on government payments will result in late fees and penalties, which are severe and should be avoided. In my experience, the IRS still has to take a back seat to essential service providers—after all, if you don't have a phone, you won't be able to do much business. But if you dig yourself into *too* deep a hole with the government, then the order of this list has to change to make the IRS your #1 priority; do what you can to keep that from happening.

3. Make any scheduled loan repayments to your bank. At some point, you may need to go back to them for more cash, and the best way to get them to help you out is if you establish a history of paying them on time.

4. Make sure your employees get paid.

5. Pay off any non-essential service providers that are likely to report you to a credit bureau and/or charge you interest and penalties if you are late. Credit cards, for example, might not harm your business if they end your account, but they can seriously damage your credit rating and keep you in a deep hole of debt by piling on late fees.

6. Pay non-essential service providers who can't or won't report you to credit bureaus in the following order:

   a. Pay the ones with whom you're likely to work often in the future and with whom want to maintain good relationships.

   b. Pay the ones who complain the loudest and most often.

   c. Pay the ones who complain the least and are more understanding about your cash-flow problems.

I know that the end of that list seems unfair; the companies who are more agreeable and understanding end up getting paid last. But unfortunately, that's the way it works. Money is a finite resource, and when you don't have enough of it to go around, you need to pay people and companies not in the order that you like them the most, but in the order that will be most beneficial to the growth and survival of your company.

77. Offer Vendors More for Delayed Payments

Most vendors will require a down payment on any project that they do for you, with the balance due either upon delivery or within 30 days of the project's completion. If you offer to pay them an extra 5 percent on top of the price you've agreed to pay, however, they may let you pay it after 90 or 180 days. This will let you use your money for other things in the short term. (Obviously, the only time you make requests like this is when you're hurting for money.) Just make sure that when the time comes to pay them off, you adhere to your end of the bargain or you could forever ruin your relationship with that vendor, and may have a hard time getting other vendors to make similar deals with you. (Word gets around fast when you don't pay up.) When I was starting my company and I was is a tenuous financial position, I used this tactic pretty often. Surprisingly, though, very few companies ever accepted the additional percentage; most just gave me more time to pay because they appreciated the offer.

78. You May Be Able to Qualify for Government Grants or Benefits

Look into federal or state government grants for which your business may qualify as a way of getting some cash into your business, additional tax deductions, or access to valuable contracts. For example, there may be grants for companies that are researching and developing new energy-efficient technologies (or at least tax credits provided to those companies that use them), open child care centers, or do marketing for local tourism purposes. Further, some grants and programs are set up for companies owned by people with a military history, the disabled, minorities, women, or people located in a geographic area that is recovering from some sort of natural disaster. For these types of businesses, one of the biggest benefits the government will provide you is access to government contracts. In addition to potentially having a high financial value, these contracts are also very safe; you're not going to have to worry too much about the government not paying you.

Think twice before deciding that you don't qualify for any of these government programs. There may be simple things you can do to become qualified. For example, suppose a male entrepreneur owns an LLC in equal partnership with a female business partner, with each one holding 50 percent of the stock. Although 50 percent may not be enough to qualify the business as female-owned (which would open the company up to government contracts), 51 percent would be enough to tip the scales. The male in the scenario can't sign over that extra 1 percent to his business partner, however; that would be the equivalent of handing over all decision-making power. (If one person owns 51 percent or more of a company, that person can outvote everyone else and have their way all the time.) Instead, the male can simply sign over 1 percent of his shares to another female who will not take part in the company's decision-making, such as his wife, mother, or sister, to qualify the company as "female owned." This opens the company to lucrative government contracts without upsetting the balance of power.

The point is, there are a number of programs out there that your company may be able to take advantage of. Although few if any of these are free money (even the grants will usually require your company to match investment dollars), they certainly can give a small company a helpful boost.

79. Don't Be Too Quick to Show a Profit

If you have investors who are specifically looking for you to quickly show a healthy profit, then skip this tip altogether. Otherwise, don't go into business believing that profit is a good goal. A big profit means a big tax burden, which is never a good thing. As much as you can—and without breaking any laws—you want to keep your profit as low as possible while still making money and/or moving your company forward in a positive direction. There are a number of ways to do this:

- If you plan to make any type of investment in your company, such as new computers, advanced purchases of inventory, etc., don't wait until next year; make them at the end of the current year. That way, you can deduct the amount of the investment this year and reap the rewards later.

- If you get new accounts toward the end of the year, hold off generating invoices until after January 1st so that the income won't apply until the following year. (You may get pushback on this from your clients, however, many of whom may want to get rid of money at the end of the year to reduce their own tax burdens.)

- If you have a C corp, pay the profits out to yourself and other shareholders as bonuses at the end of the year to avoid being taxed twice.

- If you have two companies—one that is profitable and one that is losing money—you may be able to gift funds from the profitable company to the other one and gain some tax advantages in the meantime.

- If you have children over the age of 14, it may be possible to "hire" them as employees—in essence transferring income to them to enjoy a lower tax rate.

Discuss these issues with your financial advisor, who can give you more ideas and options for gaining wealth without posting too great of a taxable profit.

80. Don't Waste Too Much Time Going After Bad Debt

One of the most frustrating things about being an entrepreneur is having clients who don't pay on time—or at all. You do the work, and then have to beg, plead, yell, and threaten to get the money your client owes you. It's not right, and it can dampen your spirit and keep you from fully concentrating on your work. Even worse, if you need the money to pay your own vendors, it can cause your company to be late making payments, potentially harming your credit score and your relationship with companies who supply you with necessary products and services.

Unfortunately, there's only so much you can do to try and get payment from a client who isn't fulfilling their financial obligations—especially if the products or services you sell have already been provided or rendered. Rather than waste a lot of time chasing money (time that could be better spent going after new business), take the following steps once a payment is officially late:

1. Send an e-mail alerting the client that they've missed a payment and politely ask when you can expect to receive a check.

2. If the payment does not arrive when promised (or if the e-mail was simply ignored), call the client directly, ask them about any open invoices, and get a firm date as to when payment will be made.

3. If no payment is received, call again. This will be the last time you call. Be polite, but this time be more firm. Explain that payment needs to be made immediately. If they are local, tell them that you are willing to stop by their offices to pick up a check.

4. If you still don't get paid, send an e-mail that if payment isn't made by a certain date, you will contact a collection agency.

5. As a last resort, hire a collection agency. These companies apply the necessary pressure and take the appropriate legal steps to get payment. Most collection agencies don't charge an up-front fee; rather, they keep a percentage (usually between 10 and 20 percent) of the money they collect.

Taking these steps will give you the best possible hope of collecting money with the least amount of aggravation. Of course, if you're in a position to take more drastic measures (depending on the kind of company you run), you can always look for other, more creative options.

I once had a small client (a one-man company) that owed my agency $10,000 for the final payment on a Web site that we built for him. It was a nice site and the client was happy, but when it came time to pay the final invoice, the excuses started: "My daughter had the flu last week," "I'm out of town for a few days, but I'll get you paid as soon as I get back," and of course the classic "I put the check in the mail—didn't you get it?" After a few weeks of silly excuses, I laid out a very simply ultimatum: I would need a check by the end of the next workday or I'd be forced to take further action. (I didn't say exactly what that "further action" would be.) Of course, 5:00 p.m. the next day came and went, and I didn't receive a check or a phone call. So at 5:01, I made a change to the home page of their Web site, replacing the original content with a large announcement that the site had been taken down because the company had refused to pay its Web-development bills, and it would be back up as soon as the bill is paid. At 5:10, I got a call from my client, who was yelling and screaming at me, demanding that I change the home page back to normal. I politely explained that I would be happy to do that—as soon as I received a check for the money that he owed my company, and not a minute sooner. With no other choice and an embarrassing message for all his clients to see, he drove two hours to hand-deliver a check for the remaining balance.

In most cases, you won't have opportunities like that. But one way or another, do what you have to do to get paid without letting it negatively affect how you run your business.

81. Keep All Receipts

Keep all receipts—even small receipts, like those for road tolls. Besides recouping your money, they prove where you were going, meaning you can also recoup your miles and gas expenses from clients you visited. As far as the IRS is concerned, receipts for meal and entertainment expenses under $75 do not have to be kept. But if a receipt is not kept (or is lost), then a log of the expense, including the time, place, and purpose, must be kept. If you're audited, these records will be important, so do your best to keep an accurate accounting of all expenses. And if you can, keep each and every receipt, including those under $75.

82. Don't Rush to Throw Anything Out

Financial transactions within your company will typically involve a good amount of paperwork, including budget statements, statements of work, contracts, purchase orders, invoices, and more. This might seem like a good reason to buy a heavy-duty paper shredder, but don't be too quick to turn your financial paperwork into confetti. Legally, your business is required to keep accounts payable, accounts receivable, banking, and budget information on file for at least seven years. Keep these records as organized as possible; in the rare instance of an audit, this is key information you'll want to have on hand.

83. Create Easy-to-Use Expense Reports

Expense reports are an important part of your financial records. Many small-business owners foolishly ignore expense reports, rationalizing that it's all money out of their own pocket anyway. That's a bad philosophy. For tax, budgeting, and accounting purposes, you need to allocate expenses so that personal and corporate funds are kept separate.

For example, say you head over to the local office-supply store and pick up $300 worth of supplies; high-quality paper, printer ink, and file folders add up quickly. You use your personal credit card to pay for it, never bothering to track the cost as a business expense, figuring that your money funds the company so there's really no difference. At the end of the month, your company shows a profit of $2,000. But it's a false profit, because the $300 in office supplies that you paid for personally was really a company expense—meaning that the actual profit is only $1,700 (the original $2,000 minus the $300 supply expense). Having an artificially high profit could cause you to budget for purchases your company actually can't afford and will increase your tax burden at the end of the year. Even if you never actually repay yourself any expenses that your company owes you, it's important to keep the numbers straight on the books.

To keep everything organized, create expense reports that are simple and easy to work with for you and for any employees you hire. Create an itemized list of the most common expenses, such as Mileage, Tolls, Parking, Airfare, Hotel, Meals, Purchases, etc. Make sure that a reason for each expense is also provided, along with the date and whether the expense should be passed off to the client. (Some expenses, such as overnight shipping, should be passed on and invoiced rather than absorbed by your company.)

If you have employees who lay out personal funds for the company (for example, many employees who travel for business are often expected to pay for their own hotels, rental cars, and other costs, with the understanding that the company will repay them later), make sure they save and provide copies of all receipts, no matter how small. You can't trust employees' memories to keep track of expenses. Also, let employees know beforehand how much you're willing to cover in terms of meals, entertainment, tips, etc. so they don't spend more than you're willing to repay. Also, let them know the time frame in which you will pay them back (usually two to four weeks). Lastly, provide employees with a limited window of time to submit their expense reports, such as three months, and warn them that other-wise, they forfeit their right to recoup their money. This isn't a sneaky way of stealing from your employees; it's an incentive to get them to do their expense reports in a more timely manner. It's not fair to you, as a company owner, to work under the impression that you've got a certain amount of cash in the bank, only to be hit with a year's worth of overdue expenses all at once.

84. Take a Salary for Yourself

In the interest of self sacrifice and for the sake of your company's financial well being, it's easy to put yourself at the bottom of the list. This usually starts with not taking a salary for yourself. Bad idea. You need to take a regular salary for yourself. If the company needs money, you can always loan the amount of your salary back to the company.

The downside, of course, is that you have to pay taxes and other fees to the government based on the salary you pay yourself, which is money you won't be able to get back. But taking a salary for your-self will show exactly how much money your company is making, which in the long run will help you budget your funds more wisely and set your pricing at a level that allows you to make a true profit. It will also help reduce the profit your company shows, in turn reducing your tax burden.

Perhaps more importantly, showing a salary will be necessary to take out any kind of personal loan later on, whether it be for a car, a home, a credit card, or what have you. Banks will always want to know your salary; explaining that you don't take a salary because the company you own can't afford it won't be a viable excuse. As soon as they see you aren't making any money, there's pretty much no way they'll qualify you for a loan.

Like I said earlier, you can always loan the money back to the company (taking it back later as an expense) if need be, but paying yourself a salary will be a necessity in the long run.

85. All Is Usually Forgiven When Everyone Gets Paid

Don't be too worried about burning a bridge with smaller vendors. There will be times when relationships are strained because you end up paying bills late, and when you're trying to get caught up and make payments, there may be bitterness or harsh words. If it goes on long enough, you may start to feel like you've wrecked a good working relationship and will need to find another vendor to fulfill your needs in the future. That's probably not the case. The truth is, when you're dealing with other small companies, everything will likely be forgiven when the final bill is paid. Small companies tend to need work badly enough that they aren't too selective when it comes to who they work with. Once your outstanding debts are paid in full, you'll be surprised by how short people's memories are. The next time you have a big project with a high price tag, you'll be back working with them and having favorable credit terms extended to you in no time.

86. Don't Be Afraid of Your Clients

As a business owner, every one of your clients is an important part of your early success. It's likely that you'll bend over backward to please them to make sure they remain your clients for a long time. Too often, that includes not wanting to antagonize them when it comes time to collect payment on completed projects or products that have been delivered. It's easy to think that if you push too hard to get paid, you'll offend your client—that it will be the end of your working relationship and you'll lose out on future revenue.

It's an understandable feeling. As a small-business owner reliant on a handful of customers to survive, you're not exactly working from a position of power. But when a client owes you money that's overdue, basically what they're doing is borrowing your money without your permission—and without expecting to pay you an interest rate. You've worked for it; it's your money. You have to get it.

I'm not suggesting you strong arm or threaten anybody. If possible, you want to get paid and still retain your client. But if getting payment is too difficult, they might not be such a great client to keep after all. Don't allow your fear of losing a client prevent you from collecting money that's owned to you.

87. Seek to Cut a Deal with the IRS

The IRS gets a bad rap. The truth is, they're really not all that bad to work with. If you owe a lot of money to the IRS, you can arrange to pay it back over a period of time. Simply call them (or better yet, have your accountant call them) and set up terms to pay a small amount of money every month or extend the amount of time that you have to pay it and pay in any increments that work for you. Depending on how much you owe, you might also be able to settle with the IRS for a one-time payment that amounts to only a fraction of what you owe.

88. You Can File for an Extension on Your Taxes

If April comes around and you find that you don't have the cash on hand to pay your taxes, you can defer payment by applying for an extension. It'll cost around a nominal amount of money to file, but it will buy you an extra few months to generate the money you need.

Filing for an extension provides a good buffer when you have cash-flow issues, but only do it if you absolutely need to. Filing for an extension doesn't eliminate the stress of paying your taxes back; it just pushes it back to a later date. And although the IRS doesn't actually say so, many accountants believe that your chances of being audited are slightly higher if you file an extension. So while it's good to be aware that you can file for an extension and I recommend doing so when cash is tight around tax time, try to pay your taxes on time.

89. Get to Know the Tax Laws; There May Be Benefits You're Missing Out On

There's no two ways about it: Taxes are boring. I've often wondered how accountants avoid going absolutely crazy. But while taxes may be boring, they can also be beneficial to your company—and if you don't spend at least a little time understanding them, you could be missing out.

"But Jay!" you'll gasp, "You've stressed a few times now the importance of hiring a good accountant—isn't that his job?" Yes, but only to a point. Your accountant is going to do what you pay him or her for, which is to balance your books and prepare your taxes. Accountants will provide some consultation, but they're not going to give you a full education in accounting. Plus, they're working off-site and have other clients besides you. They're not going to give their full attention to your company; they can only work with the information you give them. If you don't realize that certain expenses can be deducted or your taxes, you'll end up not telling them—and you'll lose those benefits.

Now, I'm not an accountant, so I'm not qualified to provide too detailed of a list of federal tax benefits that you may be overlooking. Plus, different states have different laws and incentives with regard to state taxes, so not all rules will apply to all people. But some of the things to watch out for include the following:

- There are benefits to buying or leasing your car through your company. Payments are an ongoing expense that will help bring down your taxable profit. Also, don't forget to keep track of mileage that you drive for work purposes; the IRS gives you an allowance per mile.

- If you're working from home, there will be benefits based on the percentage of your home that you designate as your office, which can then be deducted from your corporate taxes. You can also deduct a portion of home-maintenance costs.

- Depending on the economic situation, who's in local and federal office, and what type of incentives are in place, there are likely time-sensitive tax benefits you can take advantage of by taking certain actions, such as hiring a new employee, upgrading to more energy-efficient equipment, etc.

- Entertainment can mean deductions, which could allow you to expense dinners out and other similar expenses when you discuss work during the outing.

To find out more about some of the tax benefits you can enjoy by owning a small company, I recommend finding a class on business tax law, checking out the IRS's Web site (www.irs.gov), or buying the *Ernst and Young Tax Guide* each year, which you can find online or in your local bookstore.

PART 6

MARKETING, SALES, AND DEALING WITH CLIENTS

You've got your company, now tell potential customers about it! As the owner, nobody will be more qualified than you to make the sale, especially in the early days. It's not easy—sales and marketing can be time consuming and complex, and are very often the reason why many companies founded on good ideas or strong products never make it past their first year in business. Concentrate hard on improving your sales and marketing skills, and you'll be in a much better position to see your business prosper.

90. The Least You'll Need for Marketing

Marketing isn't easy, and it's not always cheap. Depending on how aggressive you want to get, there are any number of ways to reach your audience: print advertising, radio, TV, public relations, and more. But there are some basic marketing requirements for every entrepreneur:

- **A company logo.** This should be simple and easily recognizable. I recommend hiring a graphic designer with brand experience to design this for you. Make sure he or she creates the logo in a program called Illustrator, and that he or she gives you the files you need to use the logo in print and online. Along with the logo, you should also settle on a corporate font and color palette. Be aware that fewer colors and no gradients will cost less to print.

- **A Web site.** Again, unless you're an experienced programmer, you should hire a professional to take care of this for you.
- **A PowerPoint deck that explains what your company does.** This is for when you meet with prospective clients.
- **Business cards.** These don't need to be expensive. You can usually get decent cards at Staples for just a few bucks. Be aware, though, that the nicer the design and paper quality, the better impression they'll make. Make sure to include the following info:
  - Your name and title
  - The company's address, phone number, and fax number
  - Your Web site's URL
  - Your e-mail address
  - Your Twitter handle

Note that the title for this tip is "The *Least* You'll Need for Marketing". You can expect to spend a lot more to get your name out there, but use these core basics to get you started.

91. Know the Importance of Your Company's Brand

You've head the word "brand" before; you may have even used the word in conversation. But surprisingly few people really understand what a brand actually is. In fact, the concept of brand is regularly debated by professional marketers who work in the field. One definition I can quickly dispel, though, is the popular (and irritating) assumption that a brand is just a logo.

Based on my experience building brands, I've developed what I believe to the be the most basic, comprehensive definition of a brand—a definition that holds real value to any company, regardless of size or industry:

> **brand:** The sum total of all user experiences with a particular product or service, building both reputation and future expectations of benefit.

Let's break this down by looking at real-life examples:

> You have clients coming in from out of town and you want to put them up in a really lush, comfortable hotel. Are you going to make reservations at Motel 6? Of course not. Why? Because you know that Motel 6 is a low-cost, low-frills chain meant more for convenience and cost savings than for comfort and amenities.

> While traveling out of state, you pass a Pizza Hut right around dinner time. Do you need to wonder what to expect? No, because the Pizza Hut interior design, menu offerings, portions, and taste are pretty much exactly the same in every restaurant in every state.

In each case, because of the reputation of these businesses, you instinctively know what you can expect and that the experience will be the same regardless of geography—even if you've never actually visited a Pizza Hut or Motel 6. That reputation is the brand.

So where does the logo come in and why do so many people mistake it for the brand? I'll go into that in more detail later. For now, I can tell you that the logo—along with other visual and audio elements such as colors, fonts, taglines, and even musical affiliations (think "by Mennen")—is the tangible (for lack of a better word) element that provides recognition of the brand. It *represents* the brand. As soon as consumers see a logo, they can reach into their mental filing cabinet containing every brand they've ever come in direct (or indirect) contact with and establish an immediate expectation upon which to base a purchasing decision.

Of course, it's not as easy as simply being consistent in whatever product or service is being provided. Reputations and expectations must be based on *something* if consumers are going to put their trust in a brand. The elements that make up the brand and work toward building this trust include the following:

- **The promise.** Although this isn't always expressly stated, it's one of the key factors in branding. What is being promised to the consumer? Nike doesn't just make sneakers. Anyone with rubber and leather can do that. Nike is promising a better athletic and fashionable experience through use of their product. They're promising a lifestyle, where their customers will be part of an in crowd that includes sports and music stars. Do they ever come out and say that? Not that I've heard…but the promise is clearly there.

- **The personality.** Like people, brands have their own personalities. Some are quirky (think Volkswagen); others are refined (think Jaguar); and still others can range from downright silly and approachable to corporate and wise. The brand's personality creates that emotional connection that draws in a target market. That doesn't mean the brand's personality is strictly a part of the marketing process (although it's always important to market with the personality in mind). Rather, the brand's personality is something consumers come to rely on. Part of a brand's enduring reputation is how true it stays to that personality.

- **The USP (unique selling proposition).** This is the single element that makes any company, product, or service different from any other company, product, or service. It could be a distinctive recipe for ranch dressing or special quilting that makes a paper towel more absorbent. Whatever it is, every brand needs to provide at least one quality that makes it unique on the market.

As mentioned in my definition, a brand is "the sum total of all user experiences." This sum total is in constant flux, with additions and subtractions made with each consumer interaction. This is why brand building—the process of making those interactions more positive than negative—is so important. In building their reputation, brands need to not only be aware of these elements—the promise, the personality, and the USP—but consistently fulfill each one. Anytime the promise is broken, a dent is made in how the brand is perceived by the public. Anytime the brand is not true to its personality, it takes another step away from its customers and further diminishes its viability.

92. Understand What Motivates Your Customers: Brand, Price, Availability, or Something Else?

Consumers come in all shapes and sizes with their own touch points and sensibilities. What they respond to depends on the individual, product or service category, and the brand in question. Personally, I couldn't care less about paper towels; I just grab whatever brand is closest to the end of the grocery-store aisle regardless of color, price, number of sheets, absorbency, or whatever. In fact, the only factor I *do* care about is spending as little time in that aisle as possible. But offer me a Diet Coke for free or tell me I can drive five miles to buy Diet Pepsi at full retail price and I'll thank you for the offer but be on my way to buy myself a Diet Pepsi every time. My affinity for particular brands is based first on how important the category is to me (paper towel products: not at all; cola products: extremely) and second on my tastes for and experience with individual brands within that category.

In considering the target market for any brand, consumers can be segmented into five distinct groups:

- **Brand loyal.** These consumers are committed to one brand— so much so that price is rarely a factor and they'll go out of their way to get it. Very little will take them away from a brand they trust and are loyal to. These consumers are also typically eager to tell other people about their favorite brands.

- **Brand preferred.** These consumers prefer certain brands over others and will go a bit—but not far—out of their way to get them. Slight price differentials or reduced accessibility are not enough to make them change brands, but significant changes in either variable may cause them to research other options.

- **Brand aware.** These shoppers may like one brand over another—enough to recommend that brand to others if asked—but they're not that likely to go out of their way for it. Slight differentials in price or accessibility compared to competing brands might sway their purchasing decisions.

- **Brand conscious.** These shoppers do not have a preference of one brand over another, and they wouldn't go out of their way for a particular brand. Price and accessibility are often the determining factors in their decisions about which products to buy. These shoppers, however, do prefer to choose among brands they know or about which they have formed an opinion (either through direct use or reputation). They stay away from brands they don't know and avoid generic, unbranded products.

■ **Brand indifferent.** These are shoppers who base their decisions strictly on price and convenience. They are open to that they do not know and are also open to generic, unbranded products.

In maximizing their budgets, marketers should be looking to reach the "sweet center"—those people who make up the brand-preferred, brand-aware, and brand-conscious groups. These groups represent the most likely converts. Consumers who are already brand loyal don't need any further marketing; they're already convinced. As long as you don't forget them and you stay true to your brand, they'll be advocates. Consumers who are brand indifferent are also not worth spending money on. (Sorry, but no amount of money spent on marketing is going to get me to care about paper towels.) Marketers who want to increase their ROI need to target consumers who are sandwiched between these two extremes, starting with a heavy focus on those in the brand-preferred range and working down to those in the brand-conscious category.

93. Consider Geography

Is yours a service company that requires you to be on hand to oversee every project? Or is it a product-based company that could just as easily make shipments to France as it could to your next-door neighbor? Determining your boundaries will help you figure out how to run your marketing and sales programs and concentrate on getting new clients as efficiently and effectively as possible.

Make a list of your primary and secondary geographic targets and then concentrate your efforts in those areas. Otherwise, you'll end up marketing yourself blindly with no real focus. Unless you have a significant marketing budget or a large enough sales force to easily cover a wide geographic area, you'll end up diluting your efforts and revenue.

94. Don't Wait Too Long to Find New Clients

The sales process starts as soon as you decide what kind of company you want to launch. Depending on the type of business you're running and the types of clients you're looking for, the sales cycle can be very long. In my industry (marketing), getting a new small client—from the first introduction to the signed contract—will take on average three months. To secure a new large client, the average is more like nine months (and I'm probably being generous). So don't get caught flat-footed. Treat the procurement of clients as your number-one priority right from the outset. Tap into friends and family to spread the word and help you get initial clients—or at least generate some interest in your company—as early as possible. You don't want to spend money getting everything set up and then have to go through the process of coming up with a client list.

95. Long-Term Greedy Is the Best Kind of Greedy

In the 1980s, Gordon Gekko uttered the phrase "Greed is good," in one of the all-time greatest business movies ever made, *Wall Street* (later, in the last section of this book, I reference that movie as one of my motivations when I need a boost). What was so interesting about Gekko as a villain was that much of what he said made sense. Greed, as he described it—for love, money, knowledge, happiness—is good. So be greedy. After all, you're in business to create a better life for yourself, and greed doesn't always have to be just about money. But you should try to think "long-term greedy" instead of "short-term greedy." Short-term greedy will result in quick sales, but will likely not create long-lasting customers. Long-term greedy—that is, sacrificing a small, short-term gain for a far larger gain in the future—will take more patience as you grow your company, but it's the difference between a one-time sale and a client relationship that starts slowly but lasts a long time.

96. Get Involved

Look for opportunities to sit on boards or volunteer with organizations that will help promote your name and introduce you to other people. Local Chambers of Commerce are good places to look, as are local chapters of large industry organizations. Playing an active role will pay dividends, as you'll increase your profile and visibility.

That being said, realize that volunteering will require a lot of time and commitment, so make sure you're able to see it through. The worst thing you can do is offer to serve on or lead a committee and then skip meetings and fail to fulfill your promises. That will only harm your reputation, painting you as a person who fails to follow through on your commitments—not exactly the best way to build a loyal following of new customers.

97. Get Out There and Network

It's always nice to make random connections in unexpected places. I once chatted with a woman standing behind me in line at Sbarros; turned out she was the Director of Communications for a medical-device company and, later, a new client! But you also need to hit networking events. Most of these can actually be a lot of fun—you mingle, have a drink or two. But by the time you pay the fee to get in, not to mention parking, tolls, bar tabs, etc., they can also be expensive, not to mention time consuming. Clearly, you can't go to every one that comes your way, so be selective:

- Pick events that will be more lively and social.
- Events held in bars, especially in a city, tend to draw more people.
- If the event has a decent speaker, that could also be a draw for a larger crowd.

Choose events based on your goals for marketing yourself. If you're looking to increase sales, go to networking events where you can meet potential clients, not talk to people from your own industry. On the other hand, if you're looking for a new job, people within your industry are exactly who you want to hang out with. You can usually find networking events simply by checking out Google or MeetUp.com or by asking other people in and around your industry which events they usually attend.

98. Start Building Your E-Mail List

Before I start, let me just say: I am not condoning spam. Not at all. I get more junk mail in my spam folder than you would believe. I can't tell you how many times I've won some European lottery that I never entered and how much money I've apparently inherited from wealthy Nigerians over the years. But in terms of legitimate marketing efforts, e-mail marketing is a method you should actively take advantage of. For example, you might send out marketing e-mails to alert people to new blog posts you've written, Webinars or speaking engagements in which you are featured, and what have you.

With mail marketing, you can

- Send e-mails that look like Web pages, using HTML code for unique layout and design.
- Include links to your site, blog, Twitter account, and more.
- Immediately get your message in front of new, existing, and potential contacts, without a very high cost.
- Track how many people open your e-mail, when, who clicked a link, and which links clicked.

So how do you go about building your e-mail marketing list—that is, the list of contacts who will receive your e-mails? Personally, I built my e-mail marketing list from a collection of all contacts I've made. I also gather the e-mail address of anyone I'm on a CC list with and at times visit Web sites for various organizations, such as Chambers of Commerce, and copy and paste e-mail addresses for their members (assuming they're posted online) into my list. As to whether this jibes with the official laws about e-mailing promotional messages, I can't really say. I'm not a lawyer. That's something you should check out for yourself before you do anything with e-mail marketing.

One more thing: If you engage in e-mail marketing, don't make a pest of yourself. Limit contact to no more than once per week. That's usually enough to keep yourself recognizable without becoming too much of a nuisance.

99. Start a Blog

For those not totally familiar with the term, a *blog* is simply an online journal where you can record your thoughts on various topics that the public can read, share, and comment on. Having a blog for your company enables you to control the topic of conversation, demonstrate your knowledge and experience, and let potential clients see what you're all about. It's a chance to establish yourself as a thought-leader and to build a loyal following.

While there are any number of ways to start your own blog, I strongly suggest looking into WordPress.com. WordPress is one of the best resources for maintaining your own blog presence. It's free, it's quick to set up, and it's easy; you can create and update your blog without knowing a lot of code.

Like anything you do in marketing, success with blogging is more likely if you keep it going and maintain a regular schedule. Blogging can't be random, haphazard, or disorganized. To start building an audience and keep people coming back, you need to generate new content on a regular basis. Whether it's once a week, once every two weeks, or once a month (once a week is better), stay consistent and stick with it.

100. Work the Online Networks

So here's the thing about social networking: It can be time consuming, and it can take awhile before you really start seeing results. This can be frustrating, because thanks to the speed of the Web, not many people have the patience to wait for things to happen over time. The trick is to adopt social media as part of your entrepreneurial commitment, as much a part of your daily routine as showering or brushing your teeth, rather than looking at it as a chore or something you need to get out of the way. Social networking, if done right, can put you in contact with many more people than you could possibly meet otherwise, and it will play a central role in your efforts.

Consider your daily schedule and find a way to weave your online efforts into your everyday rituals to truly make the most of it. For example, my own routine is to wake up each morning, turn on my laptop, go to AdAge.com, find an article I think is interesting, read it, and leave a long comment on it. (I then copy and paste my comment into a Word document and save it on my hard drive for later use.) Then, I grab the URL for the article, shorten it using bit.ly (a Web site that enables you to reduce the length of a URL to make it easier to share), and broadcast it through Twitter, Facebook, and Linked-In. Also, throughout the day, I try to find five new people to follow on Twitter and five new people to friend on Facebook. In addition, at least twice each week, I respond to a post in a Linked-In group that I subscribe to, and at least once each week, I publish a new blog post (usually using one of the comments that I left on AdAge during the week). On top of all that, I send an e-mail blast to all my contacts once per month, letting them know about new blog posts and other information.

Of course, there is only so much time in the day, and "social media" includes so many sites, it can be tough to figure out where to start and how to fit them all in. If time is a factor (and it will be), concentrate on the "big three": Facebook, Twitter, and Linked-In. (The sites comprising the "big three" may change; social networks have a tendency to gain and lose favor without much notice. But at least at the time of this writing, these three are pretty important and are likely to play a key role in marketing oneself for some time. Learn how to use them as best as you can.) While these three are arguably the most important networks for marketing yourself, the social-media universe is a big place. There are plenty of other relevant networks, including Digg, Technorati, and an uncountable number established to serve people interested in a specific industry or hobby. Focus on the big three, but keep your eyes open and consider other networks that might help you reach your own goals.

101. Sell By Not Selling

You have your business up and running and a whole bunch of shiny, new products and services to sell. You can't wait to get out there and make your pitch! But sales don't always work that way. Sure, if you're selling sandwiches, then your market will come to you; your sales initiatives will be fairly straight-forward and direct. But if you're selling a service or a larger product that's more of a want than a need or that requires you to compete against others to land an account, then it can't be all about you.

Having a client is like building a relationship—and sales is the facilitation of that relationship. Any relationship takes a certain amount of give and take; as much as you may want to be out there selling your company, you're going to want to exercise some restraint. See what other people's needs are and look for ways to help them reach their goals. Shoot an e-mail to clients and prospects every now and then just to say hello, showing that you value them for reasons other than work. Helping people with seemingly selfless acts or just being friendly will pay dividends in the future. I'm not talking about karma; I'm talking about the basic truism that people usually go out of their way to help those who have helped them.

102. Don't Offend or Alienate Your Prospects or Clients

Religion and politics are always volatile issues, and can create lines of division that are difficult to cross. People often take both topics very personally and are easily offended if they feel their opinions and beliefs are attacked. Remember: No matter how firm you are in your convictions, others may not agree. Be careful not to offend with what you feel is nothing more than a casual addition to a conversation.

As an example, consider the following:

> New contact: So, how's business been?
> You: Not bad. The government is doing everything it can to raise our expenses, but we're getting through!

Believe it or not, this kind of exchange happens all the time. The marketer, so sure in his or her own belief, simply assumes that the new contact feels the same way. But that's not a guarantee; if the new contact has a different viewpoint, the conversation will either lead to an uncomfortable debate or end abruptly and awkwardly. Avoid this by eschewing politics or religion as a topic of conversation until you get know the person better.

103. Do Something Different to Stand Out

What are you bringing to the party? What do you have, say, or know that's going to make you stand out and make people want to connect and stay connected? If you want to stand out, you need to be unique—offer some insight, knowledge, creativity, experience, angle, service, product, or wisdom that people will be interested in and unable to find elsewhere. Even further, if you do something specific that separates you from the crowd, you'll find yourself more in demand. Write a book, contribute articles to a popular print or online publication, or record a series of Web videos that get people's attention. Get your MBA or, better yet, your doctorate. Hold a seminar. Write a white paper on some industry issue. Whichever route you take, produce or accomplish something that shows you've attained some level of success and knowledge.

104. Speak Up

Obviously, speaking is a central part of marketing yourself and your company. Indeed, speaking publicly is one of the best ways to get new clients. When you do, you show yourself off as an expert and enable prospective clients to come to you. But it's also one of the more difficult talents to master. Personally, I still struggle with speaking well. I think the word I've head most often in my life is, "What?" because for many years it was simply impossible to understand a word I said because I spoke so quickly. (Fortunately, this is no longer the case, but it's taken a good amount of work to overcome it.)

When speaking to others, whether one on one or to a group, remember the following:

- Enunciate your words.
- Keep your chin up when you speak. It will help you enunciate.
- Don't mumble. Speak up and speak clearly.
- Slow down. Don't trip over words, and don't be afraid to pause between ideas.
- Be engaging. Believe in your words, and speak with conviction.
- Use inflection and body language to emphasize your points.
- Pay attention to what you're saying. It's common for people to think ahead to their next thought before finishing with the current one, the result being that the speaker has a hard time finding his or her words.

Speaking well takes practice. Buy a digital recorder and record yourself speaking, then play it back and listen for the problem areas. Once you get the hang of it and you start to feel comfortable, look for opportunities to speak publicly at local colleges and industry associations.

105. Tap Into Your Clients' Clients

Build relationships with your clients' clients whenever you can. For example, suppose you own a small video-production company that writes, shoots, and edits corporate videos and commercials, and one of your clients is a local magazine that happens to be doing profiles on local businesses in the area. You might offer to videotape head shots of personnel of each of the businesses that will be profiled at cost (which the publication can use for promotional purposes)—provided that the taping is done at your own studio. Sure, you'll lose some money on the production, but you'll suddenly have lots of local business owners visiting your studio. When they do, give them a full tour of your place and one of your media kits. It's a great way for you increase exposure, and it will only take one or two resulting productions to make the venture profitable.

106. Promises Don't Pay the Mortgage

Don't get sucked in by a potential client who wants you to give them lower prices because they promise to introduce you and your company to other potential clients. (This is different from promising that they'll give you more work; it's completely reasonable for a company to evaluate the quality of your work before spending a fortune. Just be prepared for the possibility of setting a bad precedent if you give in too easily or settle for too low of a price.) If you are providing any kind of service, you'll get that offer thrown at you time and again. It rarely works out the way it was promised. Good clients will pay you a price that both of you are comfortable with and will pass your name on to people they know because you've done a good job—not dangle potential contacts in front of you like a carrot as a means of ripping you off.

107. Reach Out and Touch Someone—Over and Over Again

Looking to increase sales? Get on the phone! There's no doubt about it: Cold calling is tough. But it's often the best option for small companies trying to find new clients.

Keep the following in mind when you call:

- Thanks to the popularity of automated phone systems, there are fewer receptionists than there used to be—but they're still out there, as are personal assistants for higher-level execs. Be nice to these people. They are the gatekeepers—the ones who can put your call through.

- Know who you're calling and find the right way in. Often, the best way to get into a company is not by targeting the key decision maker but by targeting one of his or her influencers.

- Many execs get to work early, while their assistants don't arrive until after 9 a.m. Calling before someone's assistant arrives could give you a shot at reaching your contact directly.

- Don't be pushy. Be mindful that your prospect's time is valuable and that he or she likely deals with cold callers all day long. Sometimes, the best you can hope for is to be invited to call back again in the coming weeks.

- Be enthusiastic.

- Have something to offer that's valuable. Look for an interesting angle to pique your prospect's interest and make that person *want* to talk to you.

I did a lot of cold-calling in my early days, and my odds of success were pretty long. After all, I was fresh out of college with an economic degree. I had no experience in marketing and no portfolio—really, no reason for *anyone* to hand over their marketing account to my one-man agency. To get through the door, I needed to focus my prospects' attention on my skills, not on my past experience (or lack thereof). My solution: I collected magazines and newspapers from the surrounding area and found all the ads that I thought weren't particularly well done. Then I called those companies, asked for the marketing director, and explained to him or her that while I liked his or her company's ad (*never* criticize anything before you know who worked on it; the last thing you want to do is insult a prospect or his or her friends or family), I thought it might have more impact with a different layout. Then I explained—and this was key—that I had already taken the liberty of redesigning the ad and asked if I could come in and show what I had done. That got them curious! And it led to a meeting about 50 percent of the time. Of course, I hadn't *really* redesigned the ad, but I made it a point to schedule our meeting about two weeks out to give myself time. The result was I was able to focus their attention on what I could do for *them* rather than on what I had already done for others.

108. Break the Ice: Send Something Before You Call

One of the hardest parts of cold calling is getting the conversation started. I mean, what do you say after, "Hello, may I speak to…"? It's not easy. So give yourself a reason to call. Send your prospect a brochure about your company, a small promotional item (if you go online, you can find all sorts of companies that sell pens, calendars, and other inexpensive items with your logo imprinted on them), or even a short letter introducing yourself and your services. Then wait a few days and call to make sure they've received your mail. It'll make it easier to get a conversation started and you can ease into your sales pitch from there.

109. Don't Be Discouraged By Rejection

Rejection and sales go hand in hand. You're not going to land every prospect you try to get; you're not even going to land half of them. If you're lucky, you'll land one out of every ten. Have a thick skin, don't take it personally, and be prepared to hear a lot of people say no. It goes with the territory—but it makes the word yes that much sweeter.

110. Read Your Clients' Body Language

Clients will usually let you know whether they're engaged in your sales pitch long before they speak. If you see that your prospect is getting bored or is clearly not interested in what you're showing them— they're folding their arms, sitting back in their chair, looking at their watch, checking their e-mail, etc.—then change direction. There's no law that says you have to follow a script or your PowerPoint deck just because it's there. Shake it up and move on to something they might find more interesting. Likewise, if their body language tells you that you've touched on a point or a service that seems particularly interesting to them, then go off script and explore that point. Play it up and create more interest.

111. Talk Less and Listen More

Successful salespeople aren't salespeople at all. They're problem solvers. Bottom line: You won't be able to find out what your prospects' problems are if you aren't listening to them. Hear them out. Find out what they need. Figure out how your company can help them. Then you can talk.

112. Remember Names and Faces

Claiming that you're not good with names or faces just doesn't cut it in business. Make yourself good at both. Whether it's a sales prospect, a creditor, or a banker, forgetting someone's name or failing to recognize that person altogether is a sure-fire way to turn him or her off immediately.

113. Be Personable and Charismatic

Getting ahead means being good with people. Learn to be charming. Ask questions and be interested in the answer. Speak less and listen more. People love to hear themselves speak, and usually won't miss a chance to tell you their life story. Read between the lines; you can learn a lot about someone's personality by the way he or she speaks. Be polite and attentive. Stay in contact just to say hello. Be humble. The more people like you, the more opportunities you'll have. Don't be afraid to approach someone at a social event and just say, "Hi, my name is…." Generally speaking, people don't bite.

114. Be Prepared, and Don't Be Late

A quiet but strong sign of disrespect is to show up late to a meeting with a client or a prospect. Don't do it. Heavy traffic and getting lost are pretty weak excuses. If you don't have a GPS system, then make sure you get directions online (I'm not a huge fan of MapQuest; I prefer Google or Yahoo!, both of which are usually a little more accurate), and leave for the meeting with plenty of time to spare.

Similarly, make sure you have everything you need. The only thing worse than showing up late is showing up unprepared. Remember to bring the following:

- Business cards. It's amazing how many time people leave these at the office.
- A pad and pen for taking notes. Even if you aren't a note taker, pretend for the client's sake.
- Your company's brochure, if you have one.
- If you're making a presentation of your services, make sure you bring a printed version of it for your prospect to look through more closely after you leave. You can get these bound nicely at Staples or Kinko's for just a few dollars.
- A calendar. This can be on your phone, on your laptop, or wherever. This enables you to set a date and time for a follow-up meeting before you leave.

People want to work with companies that have their act together. Don't make a bad impression by showing up late or unprepared.

115. Anticipate Hard Questions Before the Meeting

You know your company. You know what you do, how well you do it, and what benefits a company will derive from working with you. But just because it's clear to you doesn't mean it'll be obvious to everyone. Don't be caught off guard by tough, unexpected questions. Spend a little time in advance thinking about the possible questions that will come up during your meeting and figure out beforehand how you'll answer them. In the event you are asked a question that you don't know the answer to, don't be afraid to say so. There's usually nothing wrong with saying, "I'm not really sure; let me check on that when I get back to the office, and I'll let you know." It's usually better than giving the wrong answer or struggling to come up with something and looking like you're floundering.

116. Get Prospects to Buy In

One of the best ways to close a deal is to get a prospect to buy in. What I mean is, get their opinions first and try to find a way to work those opinions into the product or service you're selling them. Everybody likes to feel that their thoughts are important and that they've somehow influenced the world around them. By making them part of what you're selling, you'll greatly increase your chances of closing the deal.

117. Don't Be Afraid to Say No

Don't be afraid to say no to an account. Some projects take too long to complete or just aren't worth the money you can make on them. While you might be tempted to take every project that comes your way because you need the cash, you may end up regretting it in the long run.

There are a number of reasons you might want to reject an account or client:

- You're positive that you can't do the job due to lack of time, talent, or budget.
- You suspect that the client will make a lot of non-chargeable changes during the course of the project.
- You get the feeling that you'll have a hard time collecting payment from the client.
- The project you've been asked to do won't keep your interest and you'll dread having to work on it each day.
- The project will take you far from your core services in a direction you're not dedicated to pursuing.

118. You Can Succeed and Be Honest at the Same Time

Don't believe that dishonesty is the only way you can achieve success. It's not true. Of course, you may have to tell a few white lies along the road to success, and there may be times when you'll need to exaggerate your company's size or experience. But you don't need to go beyond that.

You can be as successful as anybody else without having to be dishonest. That means don't cheat or con people out of money, don't try to cheat on your taxes, don't bait-and-switch (in other words, don't advertise one product at one price with no intention of selling that product at that price), don't prey on innocent people, don't generate fake invoices, or take any measures that fall into any of these categories. Even if someone offers you cash to do a large project as an incentive to charge them less (because they assume that you won't pay taxes on cash), remember that by accepting, you are essentially stealing from people like your family, friends, and other honest, hardworking folks.

A while back, I was in a café, talking with some friends who were launching a landscaping business. They showed me some photographs of their work, and it caught the attention of the man sitting at the next table. He asked questions about their work, so they started chatting. Good for them! Any new contact can be a good new contact. At some point during their conversation, one of my friends said something like, "We just got started; we're just a couple people trying to build an honest business doing something we love." To which the man replied, "Well, that's your first mistake. You can't be honest in business if you want to be successful." The sad part was, he wasn't joking. He sincerely meant it.

Anyway, they talked a bit more, exchanged business cards, and the man left. My friends were very excited; they had just met a new potential client! But I wasn't so thrilled for them. I told them that I thought it was great that they were able to meet and talk to a stranger so easily—very important when growing a business—but that they should throw out his card and never do business with him. Anyone who brags about the importance of dishonesty in business, I explained, is someone who won't hesitate to bounce a check—if he ever pays you at all. Skipping to the end of the story: They didn't listen, and a year after completing work for this man they're still trying to get their money.

Be honest, be real, and keep your eyes open for those who aren't.

119. Be Strategic in Your Sales

Being honest doesn't mean you can't be aggressive and take measures that will increase your business. Case in point: Numerous times when my agency was still very small, a large prospective client would visit our office for a meeting and to check out our company. They wanted to see that we were active and legitimate. Realizing that five employees, including myself, simply wasn't going to cut it, I reached out to friends and friends of friends, offering $20 to anyone willing to spend a few hours sitting at an open desk pretending to work, walking past the conference room with files, and otherwise acting like they were doing something important. If there were any empty desks left over, I covered them with office supplies and framed pictures and draped jackets over the empty chairs to make it look like the people who regularly occupied those workstations simply weren't there at the moment. By the time our prospect arrived, the office would be jumping with activity; even I would be convinced we were bigger than we really were!

I don't believe you need to cheat or steal to become successful. But there's a big difference between dishonesty and strategic selling. Don't be afraid to take measures that give your company a certain appearance or help you get a new client, as long as those measures don't cross the line.

120. Create the Illusion of Grandeur

If your company needs to look bigger, expand your presence to another city. It's easy to do—just get a P.O. box somewhere and have the mail that goes there forwarded to your main address, or get an 800 number for all offices with the calls being directed to your local one. You might not market your company in those other cities or even have any interest in doing business there, but being able to say that you have a presence elsewhere gives the impression that you are larger than you really are.

121. Many Variables Go Into Smart Pricing

Most business owners are ready to give away the farm to get a new client. Don't. Think carefully about what you charge to make sure that the price you come up with is fair to both you and your client. Your clients need to receive value for the price they're paying, and you need to feel adequately compensated for the product or service you're providing.

When putting together your price points, consider the following:

- What the competition is charging. You won't always know this, but if you keep tabs on your competitors, you'll start to get a sense of how they price themselves.

TIP If your company provides services, don't print and distribute a price sheet or post prices on the Web. That gives competitors a glimpse of what you're charging, not to mention locking you into a price unnecessarily.

- What the market will accept. Especially when it comes to services, you can typically charge larger companies more than smaller companies for the same service, simply because they're larger and can afford more.
- Your costs of doing business. These include more than just the hard costs you have to pay to create a product or provide a service; they also include the hard costs of materials needed for a product or service as well as employees, taxes, and overhead (rent, office materials, phone bills, etc).
- Your profit.

All these things need to be taken into consideration when you come up with a price for your product or service, as well as the volume you need to sell at that price to generate revenue.

122. Don't Sell Yourself into a Downward Spiral

The rent is about due on your office space and you don't have the cash. Worse, you haven't established a relationship with a bank yet and there's no way you're going to qualify for a credit line quickly enough to make the payment. What do you do?

If you're like many entrepreneurs, you do the wrong thing: You undersell a product or service to get some quick cash. Suppose, for example, a service you provide would ordinarily sell for $5,000. You decide to cut your price in half to get a new client to sign on with you immediately, asking for a 50-percent deposit. So you've sold the service for $2,500, and you've got a check in hand for half of that. That will cover the rent payment that you owe, solving your immediate problem—but without realizing it, you've created far larger problems for yourself down the line.

Let me explain. Suppose that between materials and time, this project will cost you $4,000. At the original, standard price, you would have waited longer to get an account, but you would have profited $1,000. Instead, you undersold it, taking a $1,500 loss in order to generate immediate cash. Not far down the road, that loss will rear its head in the form of bills that need to get paid. To pay them, you'll likely sell *more* services at discount rates, collecting more immediate cash, but increasing your future debt/losses. It's a downward spiral that can have a very unhappy ending if you allow it to continue.

Rather than continuing to sell products and services at a loss, you're better off delaying payments to certain vendors. In the case of this example, you should call your landlord, explain the situation, and ask for an extension. If your landlord says no, well, don't pay him or her anyway. It's unfortunate, but you're not going to be kicked out for being late one time. In addition, find other payments you can hold off on. Use credit cards for certain purchases to save cash in the short run. All these are better options than taking a loss for immediate cash.

123. Watch the Precedents That You Set

If you are building a service-oriented company, you may be tempted to provide your service to an early client at a low price. Many new service companies use this strategy to land a sale, assuming they will keep the client for a long time and make up the money with future sales. While this will help you start building an early client list for your business, be aware that once you set a precedent with a client by offering a very low price, it will be highly unlikely that this client will ever allow you to raise prices for future services to the appropriate level. So if you're not prepared to keep prices at the ultra-low level, get ready to lose those early clients more quickly than you'd expect.

When I first started my agency, I had a chance to build a Web site for a division of a large company. To get the job, I charged $10,000 for what should have been a $50,000 project. A year later, another division of the same company wanted to hire me to build their Web site. When I gave them a quote of $70,000 (a very fair price), they balked. They couldn't justify $70,000 when the other division had only paid $10,000.

124. Get Clients to Cover All Hard Costs

Although you don't want to nickel and dime your clients, you should keep track of external hard costs that you incur for them and make sure they get invoiced. Overnighting a letter via Fed Ex, for example, can cost $17 a pop. After a while, that adds up; make sure your clients get billed accordingly. Other hard costs, like travel expenses or materials needed to complete a job, should also be recovered. Make sure it's clear in your initial proposal and contract that hard costs will be billed separately to the client. And don't be afraid to tack on an additional percentage for handling; 10 to 20 percent isn't unreasonable or unusual.

All that being said, don't go overboard. I don't know too many companies outside the legal industry, for example, that charge for each photocopy they make. I recently killed a $100,000 proposal from a company for services because they wanted to charge me 35 cents per mile to drive to my office for meetings. Riiiiight.

125. Get Invoices Out to Clients Quickly

Many companies won't honor invoices submitted more than 90 days after the service was provided, so make sure you bill your clients within that 90-day window. Not only will it improve your cash flow, you'll find that smaller customers will have a tough time paying you if you send them a bill for services accumulated over a long period of time.

When you and your financial planners prepare your accounts-receivable statements, break them up into categories of Current, 31–60 Days Overdue, 61–90 Days Overdue, and Over 90 Days Late. This will give you an indication of how much money is owed to you overall, how much of it is coming in late, and so on. If many of your customers are individuals or small companies, be careful to avoid allowing them to slip out of the 31–60 Days Overdue category. The longer they go without paying, the less likely you are to ever see the money at all.

By the way, for budgetary purposes, you should assume that any-where from 5 to 10 percent of your accounts receivable will go unpaid. That's not necessarily a bad thing; getting paid 100 percent might indicate that your prices are too low.

126. Get Signatures and Purchase Orders

Get signatures on every contract or proposal *before* you begin to work on it, and create purchase orders for product-related transactions. Don't do any work until you have an agreement with your client in writing—preferably with a deposit.

PART 7

FINDING AND MANAGING EMPLOYEES

As your company grows, you may be expected to wear many hats. But inevitably, there will be skills required that you just don't have. Hiring a workforce can help you fill in those gaps. In fact, you may find that you *must* hire employees to achieve any real growth. But with each employee you hire, you'll evolve from "owner" to "boss" or "manager"—and that can be a tough transition to make. The following tips should point you in the right direction.

127. Understand the Importance of Hiring Employees

Hiring your first employee is a big step, and a big commitment:

- It's a commitment to the government; you're going to need to start paying payroll taxes, Social Security, federal and state tax withholdings, and more.

- It's a commitment to your employees, who are going to be spending their time and effort to improve your company.

- It's a commitment to your company, your contribution to it, and how it will operate moving forward.

So why do it? The easy answer is simply that you need help. You get busy enough that eventually, there is too much for any one person to do—yes, even you—and you need other people to help get the work done. The longer answer is that entrepreneurs who work on their own will usually find themselves in a dangerous wave pattern. Imagine a continuous line that goes up, reaches a peak, curves back down, reaches a low point, and then curves back up again—endlessly. That's the way business is typically run when it's a one man show. You're responsible for everything, so you're off doing sales and bringing money into the company. That's the up part of the wave. The wave hits its peak when you land some new clients. Then, your time is taken on service and production as you start to work on those new projects or fill those orders. But while you're doing the work you've been hired to do, you're not doing any more sales, so the wave moves downward until the projects are complete and the wave can move upward again as you go back to doing sales.

The ideal is for the peaks and valleys in the wave pattern to become less severe, eventually becoming a straight line with an upward-moving slope. That will only happen, though, when you run sales and production efforts simultaneously—tough to do when you're the entire company. So you hire employees to fill in the gaps and make the wave less severe.

The trick is knowing which pieces of work you want to give up and which pieces you want to keep for yourself. Here's where you need to be honest with yourself and assess where your true talents lie. My first hire was easy: I hired a woman to be an office manager/receptionist/bookkeeper. Those were jobs I didn't want to do on my own and wasn't particularly good at. By hiring someone else to take them over, I was able to make my company's wave pattern less severe because I could dedicate the time my employee was saving me to both sales and output. It was hiring my second employee that was problematic. As a small marketing agency, most of the early projects I sold were design based: brochures, local ads, logos, things like that. To straighten my wave pattern a bit more, I needed to either hire a salesperson and concentrate on design or hire a graphic designer and concentrate on sales. I enjoyed designing more than I enjoyed selling, but when I was honest with myself, I had to admit I was better at sales than I was at graphic design. So I hired a designer and hit the road in search of new clients.

Of course, the wave pattern never completely turns into a straight line; there are always a few bumps and dips along the way. But if you hire the right people, you'll find that the endless cycle of ups and downs will turn into more steady, reliable growth.

128. Interns Can Provide Inexpensive Help

Okay, so maybe they're not the most experienced people, but students are often among the most motivated, hungry employees you can ask for. Plus, they're inexpensive. Many will work simply for course credit (although I believe paying interns at least a few dollars an hour will keep them motivated and appreciative). Contact the career-placement office at local colleges to find out how you can get new interns each semester.

Don't think that just because they're young, all interns will be good for is getting you lunch. Over the years, I've worked with many interns who have been proactive and creative, done some stellar research for upcoming presentations, helped assemble proposals, and even managed some small public-relations work. Very often, a good intern can turn into a great employee after graduation.

129. There Are Many Ways to Find New Employees

It may seem that the only way to find qualified employees is to go through an employment agency. Not true. While it'll be harder to find qualified people if you don't use an agency, the extra work is probably worthwhile when you consider the cost of hiring an employment firm—usually somewhere around 20 percent of the hired person's first-year salary. Sure, this fee is negotiable, but even then it still adds up.

Especially with a small business, you're not going to want to shell out the extra dollars for an employment company. Instead, consider the following methods of finding good employees:

- Use your existing resources. Everyone knows someone; ask your current employees (as well as your clients) to recommend people who may be looking for work. Depending on how desperate you are, you might even go so far as to offer a monetary bonus for recommending candidates (payable upon the candidate being hired, of course). This will be far less costly that hiring an employment agency.

- Craigslist.com can be a great resource for finding employees. If you're not familiar with the site, Craigslist is the online equivalent to the Classified section of a newspaper, where people can post all sorts of ads to buy and sell items, look for a date, or find a job. In some larger cities, such as New York, there'll be a nominal fee (something like $25) for posting a job opening, but otherwise Craigslist is free. The best part is that it keeps your company's name and contact information confidential, so you won't have anxious job seekers calling you or faxing you their resume all day. My own company has found some excellent employees through Craigslist over the years and continues to do so.

- Use your Twitter, Facebook, and especially your LinkedIn networks to get the word out when you have job openings.

- Often, you'll find yourself on a friendly basis with the owners of competitive companies; inevitably, you'll meet them through networking events and so on. When you need to increase your staff, call them to see if they can recommend someone or if they can pass along some resumés to you. Even if the information they provide doesn't end up being any help, it's fun to let them know you're growing and struggling to keep up with the influx of work! As a small marketing agency in New Jersey, my company has always had plenty of competition, and over the years I've forged friendly relationships with some of my fellow agency owners. A few years back, I called the president of one agency and told him we were looking for a new business executive. The timing was right—he was about to let one of his own new business executives go. We snatched her up, and she's done a great job for us. It never hurts to ask!

There are people out there who are anxious to find a new job. Finding them doesn't have to take a lot of time or money—it just requires knowing where to look.

130. Consider Freelance Help Before Hiring Permanent Employees

I have never been a fan of using freelance help, preferring to work with full-time employees. But freelance or temporary help has many advantages of which, as a business owner, you need to be aware.

Consider the list of pros and cons for yourself before deciding which route is right for you.

Benefits of Using Freelance Help

- You only pay for the hours you need. Suppose you get a large project from a client and you need someone to help you complete part of it. It's a considerable amount of work, but not enough to cover 40 hours or more each week—and you're not sure you'll need the extra person once the project is finished. A freelancer can work the hours you need him or her to work without any expectations of continued employment after the project is finished.

- You can find a freelancer who is highly specialized to provide a service for a client request, even if you don't want to sell that particular service as a core part of your company.

- Hiring freelancers won't require you to pay payroll taxes, Social Security, or other such expenses to the government, resulting in a cost savings.

- You don't have to provide any of the standard benefits to freelancers that you might offer full time employees, such as health insurance or a 401(k) plan.

- If you aren't happy with a freelancer, it's relatively easy to stop working with him or her and find someone else.

- The cost of using a freelancer is a business expense that you can write off on your taxes.

Drawbacks of Using Freelance Help

- Per hour, you'll pay them far more than you'd pay a full-time employee. Taking a page from my industry, a standard salary for a full-time graphic designer with some talent and experience would be about $50,000. Based on a 40-hour week, that comes to just over $24 per hour, not including taxes, fees, and benefits. A good freelancer, on the other hand, could easily charge $40 or more per hour, cutting into the profit margin of a particular project.

- Freelancers will always feel disconnected from the company—and if you have other employees, it will be tough to create a team atmosphere in the office. This can be detrimental to morale, which is an important part of running a successful company.

- Because they don't have a true vested interest (other than the hope of being hired again for projects in the future), a freelancer will likely be less motivated than full-time employees to do an outstanding job.

- Freelancers are less likely to be loyal to your company and may end up working for competitors. Moreover, there's nothing stopping a freelancer from simply not showing up one day if a better opportunity comes along. It's unthinkable and unprofessional, but it happens.

- Full-time employees will, over time, come to know and understand your clients in such a way that they can complete projects for them quickly and more accurately. Freelancers will never fully understand your clients that intimately.

- If you work with an agency that provides you with a freelancer, they may require weekly payments rather than every other week. That can be a serious strain on resources.

To some extent, deciding which way to go is a matter of both personal preference and your current need. As I said earlier, I tend to be a big believer in the benefits of team building and corporate morale, so I prefer full-time employees to freelance help, but that's just a personal preference. One thing I do recommend, however, and often engage in myself, is hiring people for certain positions on a freelance basis for a short period of time before taking them on full time. That way, you can test their skills and see how well you work together before investing too much into them.

131. Hire People Who Are Smarter and Better Than You Are

Want to know how to tell you're successful? It's not by how much money you have in your bank account. No, you'll know you've built a successful company when it no longer needs you to function on a day-to-day basis. If you can step away from the vehicle and feel confident that it will still run on its own, *that* is an achievement to be proud of.

The hard part about achieving that goal? The only way to reach it is to swallow your pride and hire people who are smarter and better than you are at certain things. You'll always be the visionary; the company will always be your baby, sprung from your ideas and hard work. But don't feel like you always have to be the best at everything in your company to keep your place as top dog. Hire people who can perform certain functions better than you can.

My company has been around since 1994 primarily because I've done just that. The employees who have filled every position we've ever had open have performed their jobs better than I can. Our project managers are more organized than I am. Our graphic designers are more artistic than I am. Our salespeople are better at sales than I've ever been. The company still needs me to be its figurehead, to meet with our larger clients and show them some love, and of course to set the direction for growth, but on a day-to-day basis, the company can function just fine without me. It's taken on a life of its own because I've never been afraid to hire people who can outperform me. Do the same, and you'll see your company grow as well.

132. Personality Is Important

When you're interviewing new employees, trying to decide who to hire, look beyond talent and experience. Clearly, these qualities are important, as are willingness to learn, attention to detail, and any number of other traits. After all, entire books have been written about the best way to conduct interviews and how to decide which candidates are best for your company, so I'm not going to try and force fit all that content into a single tip. But what I will tell you—and in my experience, this has been true time and time again—is that personality is perhaps the single most important quality you should consider when hiring a new employee. This is especially true for small businesses, where the office space is more intimate and it's likely that any employee at some point or another will have contact with your clients.

The fact is, experience comes with time, and many talents can be taught. But if you don't like the person you're working with day in and day out, then work will be a miserable experience for everyone and productivity will suffer. Each new employee you hire needs to reflect the personality of your company and be someone with whom you will genuinely enjoy working. That's not to say you should hire anyone who comes along just because you think you'd enjoy having a beer with him or her; it just means your company will be harmed if you hire somebody you don't really like simply because you're impressed with how talented that person is. There needs to be a good balance to make the working relationship thrive.

133. Happy Employees Create a Productive Workforce

In the first section of this book, I discussed the difference between playing the part of an executive and really being one. One of the key differences is that people who play executive like to show that they are the king by treating their employees like peasants. It comes down to a basic question: Are you in business to stroke your own ego or to generate profit and build a strong company? If your answer is the latter, then the best way to go about that is to motivate your employees, make clear that you value their contributions, and generate loyalty to you and your company. There are many ways to do this:

- **Give your employees a voice.** Good managers and business owners learn from their employees. Listen to their opinions and encourage feedback. You'll always get the best work out of people who are free to speak their minds and honestly feel like their opinion matters.

- **Give compliments when they are deserved.** Surprisingly, more money isn't always as important to an employee as having their hard work verbally recognized. Let your employees know that you think their work is valuable. A simple "Hey, you're doing a great job" is usually all it takes to keep someone motivated to continue working better.

- **Ease up a little.** Don't make a big deal about rules like when employees come in or leave and how often they take cigarette breaks or make personal phone calls. Let them work in peace, without being watched over too closely.

- **Have a little fun!** Make sure work isn't always all about work. Throw parties for employee birthdays or your company's anniversary. Take all your employees out for ice cream or for a spontaneous lunch on the company. It's those kinds of gestures that will make your employees like working for you.

▪ **Be in a good mood.** Your employees will take their cue from you. If you're in a bad mood, chances are they'll be more quiet, more reserved, and more anxious about coming to you with problems, issues, and ideas. Conversely, if you're in a good mood, the entire office will be happier, more open, and more productive.

▪ **Lead by example.** You're the boss, so you need to set an example and not give your employees a reason to resent you. Coming in every morning at 10 a.m. and leaving by 3 p.m. sends a signal that the company isn't very important to you. Spending all day in your office with your door closed sends a signal that you don't want to be part of the team. Watch the signals you're sending and make sure they are positive ones.

▪ **Recognize extra effort.** If your employees are full time and are paid a salary instead of an hourly wage, you're not obligated to pay them for staying late or working overtime. But it's still a nice gesture to do something for them, even if it's just buying them pizza and soda or beer if they are staying really late. A few small (and relatively inexpensive) gestures like these will make employees feel appreciated, and they won't mind staying late to get things done.

▪ **Keep employees informed.** Do you have a good lead on a new client? Tell your employees about it. Share good news and celebrate wins with the team so that they can feel like they're part of it, and not left in the dark.

▪ **Don't flaunt your wealth.** Finally, your investment is paying off, and you're starting to make a lot of money. Enjoy it—but don't flaunt it in front of your employees by bringing them outside to see your brand new Lexus or telling them about your upcoming ski trip to France. Not a lot of people will be motivated to work hard if they're led to believe that the only reason they're waking up in the morning is to make you wealthier.

These points shouldn't be interpreted as "You should be a pushover when it comes to your employees." Far from it. You're paying their salaries; they need to produce. If they're struggling, you need to deal with those issues firmly but fairly. Being a leader sometimes means being an authoritarian when it's called for, but that's a far cry from being a dictator. Create a happy work environment where employees look forward to going, and your productivity will skyrocket.

134. Provide Benefits That You Can Afford

As this book is being written, a recession is in full swing and the unemployment rate is quite high. Under these conditions, simply having a job and a source of income is enough for many people. That's not always the case, though. As the unemployment rate falls, more jobs become available, and employees are in greater demand, you'll have to offer more to entice quality people to work for you. As a small company, you may have to make the offer particularly attractive, as many employees will view working for you as somewhat of a risk (smaller companies being in greater danger of going out of business more easily than larger, more established companies).

Typically, companies entice quality job seekers to work for them by offering a benefits package (along with a competitive salary). A benefits package can include any of a number of line items, which may be an expensive burden to you, including:

- **Some sort of health-care coverage for which you, the employer, pay some or all of the costs.** There are many plans to choose from, with the better plans being more expensive. The better the plan and the more of the costs you cover, the more likely you are to get better, more talented employees (but the more dollars out of your pocket, as health-care costs are high and often go up unexpectedly).

- **Non-basic health coverage, such as dental and eye exams.** Many employees give particular weight to dental coverage when deciding where to work.

- **A 401(k) plan, with a certain amount matched by the company.** These plans enable employees to divert a certain percentage of their paycheck to an investment account that is non-taxable until the time of withdrawal (usually the age of retirement). Some companies match a certain amount of their employees' contributions, increasing their retirement fund.

■ **Profit sharing.** Profit-sharing plans are programs in which employees get to share in the profits of the company, potentially earning them a nice bonus check at the end of the year. The nice thing about a profit-sharing plan is that it provides an incentive to employees to work harder and produce more throughout the year.

■ **Vacation days.** These are usually a big deal. Potential employees will want to know how many vacation days they get, how many they can take in a row, and what happens to those days at the end of the year if they don't use them. (Some companies allow those days to be added to the following year, some companies convert a percentage of unused days into dollars and give them to the employee as a bonus, and still other companies simply say that if you don't use your vacation days, you lose them.)

■ **Sick days and personal days.** These are also good benefits to potential employees.

Of course, there are plenty of other benefits that you can provide, such as reimbursement for commuting costs, memberships to local health clubs, etc. For you as a business owner, the trick is to put together a benefits package that will get quality job seekers to want to work for you but that isn't so expensive that you won't be able to afford it.

135. Create an Employee Handbook

Even if you only have a few employees, it's important to establish the rules in advance, putting them in writing so they are very clear to everyone who works for you. For your small company, the handbook doesn't have to be long, but there are certain rules and guidelines it needs to cover:

■ A signature page that each employee has to sign, acknowledging that he or she has read and understands the handbook.

■ An equal opportunity employment statement that makes it clear your company does not discriminate on any basis.

■ Rules about the use of company property, primarily related to use of computers and whether employees are allowed to use them to send and receive personal e-mails or store personal files, as well as whether they can use their workplace phone to make personal calls.

- Your company's dress code. Even if it's casual, you need to outline the boundaries. (Are ripped jeans and stained t-shirts okay?)
- Rules regarding safety and accidents in the workplace, mostly noting that it is everyone's responsibility to ensure that the workplace is safe and hazard free and the location of first aid supplies, emergency safety equipment, and exits.
- Performance reviews (discussed separately later in this section of the book).
- Working hours.
- Payroll, as in when employees can expect to be paid.
- Details of the benefits package (as discussed earlier in this section).
- A calendar of paid holidays.
- Policies regarding sexual harassment, smoking, and substance abuse.
- Reasons for termination.
- Policies regarding leave for maternity, death in the family, jury duty, school, and military service.

Have your lawyer help you put your employee handbook together. Chances are he or she will already have a template established and will just need to adjust it to your specific needs.

136. Have Employees Sign a Confidentiality and a Non-Compete Agreement

Employees will have access to certain private information that could be harmful to your company if they share it with competing companies or decide to open their own company to compete with your own. Safeguard against this by drawing up a formal contract that new employees must sign before starting work with you:

- A confidentiality agreement is a contract that states that the employee understands that he or she may be privy to confidential information (such as client names and contact info, billing rates, etc.), and that he or she agrees not to discuss or share this information with anybody not directly employed by the company.

▪ A non-compete agreement states that the employee agrees, upon termination or resignation, not to work for a competing company or begin his or her own competing company. These agreements usually place limitations on geography and time— for example, stating that an employee can't work for or begin a competing company within 200 miles and/or within two years of resignation of termination from the employer.

Once again, have your lawyer draft these documents for you. Alternatively, download a template from the Web and modify it your specific company. However you do it, getting these documents signed is important for maintaining corporate privacy and reducing the risk of unfair competition.

137. Give Regularly Scheduled Reviews

Personally, I hate giving reviews. But as a business owner, it's important to give regular reviews—in private, usually once every six months—to your employees to officially let them know how they are doing. You might use one review for information only, the other to establish what, if any, raise the employee will get. Even if you think you do a good job of letting employees know how they're doing little by little over the course of each day, having an official meeting to go over the details is essential to make things clear.

While there are many different ways to give reviews, one of the easiest is to create a list of items that are meaningful to you, your company, and the employee's position. Here's an example:

▪ Teamwork
▪ Being proactive
▪ Attitude
▪ Energy and eagerness to complete projects
▪ Ability to meet deadlines
▪ Innovation

- Attendance
- Attention to detail
- Organizational abilities

Measure each of the items on a list on a five-point scale, five being excellent and one being poor. Then create a section of the review that requires more detailed responses to questions, as in the following:

- "Where has the employee excelled?"
- "Where has the employee fallen short?"
- "In what areas does the employee need to improve?"
- "Has the employee showed improvement since the last review?"

Go through the list with the employee, explain why you gave the ratings you gave, and then go through your answers to the more detailed questions. Give the employee a chance to voice any rebuttal if he or she disagrees with any of your critiques and listen to his or her defense with an open mind. When the discussion is over, have the employee read and sign the review to verify that he or she understands and accepts it.

TIP You may also want to give employees an opportunity to openly and honestly review you as well so you know where you can improve as a manager.

---

138. To Social Network or Not to Social Network?

Today, that *is* the question—and companies of all sizes are struggling to figure out the answer. Should you allow your employees to access Facebook and Twitter on company time? What about IMing with friends? It's a tough call, and there's really no universally accepted answer to it yet.

Personally, I think that ultimately, your employees will always be the best advocates for your brand. As long as they are employed by you, they will associate themselves with your company. Rather than shutting them off from the rest of the world, allow them access to it. Give them the freedom to chat, network, and converse while at the office—with the understanding, of course, that it can't prevent them from getting their work done in a timely manner (I admit that it bothers me when I'm under a deadline and come out of my office to find one of my employees casually chatting with a friend on IM)—and possibly help to market your company a little more. I keep a close eye on things to make sure they aren't spending too much time in casual conversation, but I still allow it. The alternative is closing down their access for good, making them feel shut out from the rest of the world, and possibly encouraging them to discuss the company in a more disparaging way off hours, when I'm not around to police it.

139. Salary Employees Are Paid Yearly, Not Hourly

As a boss, you don't want to be a tyrant. You need to understand that just because you've chosen a life where work never ends doesn't mean that your employees have that same work ethic. In fact, I can promise you that you will *never* have an employee who has a stronger work ethic than you do. So don't watch the clock and give people a hard time when they leave at 5:00 p.m. on the nose; no matter how much they like their job, their *real* lives are outside of work.

At the same time, it's important that all your salary employees understand that they are paid yearly, not hourly. That means that while the workday might be from 9 to 5, if their work isn't done and deadlines need to be met, then leaving at 5 p.m. isn't going to cut it. They need to get their work done, simple as that. Don't get me wrong: I'm a big advocate of my employees being away from the office and enjoying life, to the point where I will offer to help them with their work if it means they'll get out of the office on time. But if a deadline is fast approaching or we're running behind on a project, then not staying late—sometimes very late—isn't an option. It doesn't happen often, but when it does, employees need to understand that there is no overtime pay. It's part of their job.

140. Give Salespeople Commission Plus Incentives

One of the best ways to compensate people is to pay them a base salary plus a commission or an incentive based on their performance. Salespeople, for example, typically get paid a base salary plus a percentage of net after vendor revenue.

You can even go beyond their standard commission by offering limited-time commissions based on certain types of accounts that you would like for them to bring in. For example, you could announce an extra commission percentage for any salesperson who reaches 10 percent beyond stated sales goals. If there is a particular product that is not selling well, offer salespeople a limited-time increase in commission for moving more units of that particular product.

When it comes to salespeople, more money is always a good incentive—but so is being presented with a challenge. People who have a sales mentality tend to be aggressive and motivated by overcoming obstacles. Financially, treat commissions as a vendor cost when calculating net revenue.

141. Incentivize Non-Sales Employees

Salespeople aren't the only ones who should be incentivized over and above their base salary. Non-sales staff, such as project managers, should also be given goals and rewarded for exceeding them. The bottom line is that if they don't do their jobs well, the sales staff is going to have a harder time selling. Salespeople need to know that their accounts are being properly taken care of and deadlines are being met so that they can be out there networking and finding new prospects.

"But, Jay," you say. "Why should I give an additional incentive to my employees just to do their jobs? Isn't that what I'm paying them a salary for?" It is, but human nature will likely cause them to become complacent over time. Providing an incentive to reach beyond a stated goal is a great way to motivate people to work harder. For non-sales employees, these goals should be tailored to fit the needs of your business. If you sell a product, the goal could be to produce more units per hour than the standard target output. If you're a service company, the goal can be based on completing a project more quickly (but without errors).

However you decide to measure success, make sure the goals you ask your employees to reach are beneficial to your business, and that they are challenging but still possible to attain. Also, don't go crazy with the rewards. While you'll incentivize salespeople with cash, you don't need to do the same with non-sales employees. Gift certificates, a paid day off, and other similar prizes are more than enough to do the job.

142. Micromanaging Will Keep You from Growing

Don't micromanage. Learn to let go. One of the hardest parts about growing a business is trusting others to assume responsibilities that you want to keep for yourself. In your mind, you think that nobody else can do it as well as you—and you're probably right. It's your baby, after all. But to reach the next level, you'll need to learn to let go, to trust, and to accept that even if the people to whom you give responsibility mess up now and then, everything will get back on track eventually. Delegating responsibility is a necessary step in the business-growth process.

Often, you might be reluctant to give an employee additional responsibility because that person's performance record doesn't prove that he or she can handle it. But sometimes, people do a worse job when they have less responsibility, rising to the occasion when they are given more to do. If you've ever played tennis, you'll understand this concept: When you play against a bad player, your own playing suffers. When you play against someone better than you, you play up to their level.

143. You Are Always the Office Psychiatrist

Be prepared to be the guidance counselor for many of your employees. Because you hold a position of authority, they'll often look to you for advice or will want to vent when they need to talk about events in their personal lives. In these situations, try to listen as much as possible and provide guidance without providing specific advice. Remember: You are still the boss, and getting too close is not a good idea. (Neither is providing any kind of specific advice that could turn into a lawsuit against you if it backfires.)

During the years I've had my marketing agency, I've played the doctor in more psychiatric sessions than Freud. I've heard it all: divorcing parents, inability to accept change (you gotta love those straight-out-of-college employees), broken hearts, creative blocks, you name it. Most of the time, I just nod and offer a very general response that probably won't be particularly helpful—but employees appreciate a boss who is willing to listen to them when they need to vent.

144. Expect to Be Second Guessed

It's interesting: No matter how much you accomplish, no matter how many clients you work with, and no matter how large you grow your company, your employees will always second guess you. At first, you're likely to take it personally. You won't understand why your employees don't have more faith in your decisions. But it's actually pretty healthy for them to think like that. Second guessing you—or, put another way, thinking that they can run the company better than you can—shows that they're engaged and that they care about the company. At least, that's one way to rationalize it. The point is, don't let it get to you. It's normal. Don't take it to heart and don't allow it to create a rift between you and the people who work for you.

145. Bad Behavior Is Inevitable...And Harmful

As the business owner, your primary interest is pretty singular: You want to get work done. Yes, you want to enjoy what you're doing, but ultimately, as long as your clients are happy, you'll be happy. For your employees, however, things are a little less laser focused. While they'll want to do well and keep clients satisfied, work is also a social experience for them. Eight to ten hours a day is a long time to spend with other people; clearly, not all of that is going to be filled with work-related activities. If you've ever seen an episode of *The Office*, you know that plenty goes on inside the workplace that isn't strictly work related. Interoffice romances, cliques, gossiping, and spreading of rumors are among the more typical forms of behavior that occur even in very small companies with only a few employees.

While there may not be anything you can to stop this altogether, you certainly shouldn't encourage it. In fact, whenever possible, you should try to *dis*courage it as much as possible. Why? Interoffice romances inevitably lead to breakups and difficulties working together. Cliques can dismantle teams, leaving some people feeling left out. But gossiping, often centered around the health of the company, is probably the most common—and the worst—example of bad behavior; it will inevitably result in employees worrying about problems that have at best been exaggerated or may even be fictional.

All these types of bad behavior can lead to a less productive workplace. This is where your role as the boss morphs almost into the role of a parent who needs to discipline his children. Monitor bad behavior and be prepared to talk to your employees to diffuse potentially explosive situations before they boil over and cause productivity to cease altogether.

146. Be Firm About Not Discussing Salaries

You don't want employees talking to each other about what they each make in pay. It creates an environment of envy as inevitably, one employee will wonder why another employee makes more, why a new employee is starting off at a higher level then he or she started at, and so on. In the end, nobody ends up being very happy, and productivity suffers. It's a pretty serious issue, so make it clear that if you find out they have been discussing their salaries or bonuses, they may be terminated without warning.

147. Keep Track of Employees' Hours

Time management is key to profitability. It's fairly simple math: The longer a project takes you to complete, the more that project will cost you, cutting into your profit margin. Projects that take too long will also limit the total number of projects you can work on, reducing your overall income.

But wait: It gets worse. Suppose you have one employee who earns a salary of $50,000 per year. He does good work, but he's somewhat slow—not so slow that it's obvious, but slow enough that he spends about 20 percent longer on his projects than he really has to. Currently, he's working on five client projects, each of which should take 10 hours to complete, for a total of 50 hours (10 hours × 5 projects). But because he spends 20 percent longer on each project, it takes him 12 hours to complete each one, for a total of 60 hours (12 hours × 5 projects). That 10 extra hours is the equivalent to another project that you're *not* getting paid for!

Now suppose that in the middle of all this, you get a call from a client who wants to hire your company to complete a project for them. You look at your employee, working away at his desk, and think that he is completely swamped and won't be able to handle anything new that comes along. You don't want to turn the project down, and you expect that you'll get more work from more clients in the future, so you hire a second employee, also at $50,000.

Do you see the problem? You're giving away $50,000 before you have to. If your original employee worked at a normal speed and could complete each project in 10 hours, he would have time to take on additional work, and you wouldn't have to waste money hiring someone else. In fact, if you could somehow get your employee to work even faster (see the tip in this section on incentivizing non-sales employees), finishing each project in eight hours, then you're *really* making money, and can avoid laying out additional salary expenses until much later.

The only way to get a sense of whether employees are moving too slowly is to know exactly how many hours they are spending on each project they work on. If your company is on the new side, have employees track their time on paper or in an Excel spreadsheet. As you get bigger, you can implement software that forces employees to punch in and punch out of files in order to access and work on them, giving you an up-to-the minute accounting of how time is being spent.

Once, after horribly running over on hours for a client, thereby losing a significant amount of money and causing the client to be less than impressed with our services, we looked over the timesheets of everyone who had worked on the project. We discovered that one employee in particular had spent way more time than was necessary on the project. When we asked her about it, she admitted that her boyfriend had broken up with her just after the project started and that she had spent a good amount of her time at her desk arguing with him via text message. Welcome to the world of entrepreneurship.

The point of tracking time is not to police your staff—although that will be a positive outcome. After all, you're paying them for their time, so there's no reason why you shouldn't know how they're spending it. The point is to gain an understanding of why some projects take longer than they should so you can avoid those problems the next time around, as well as to get a sense of how long each project *should* take so you can accurately price them out in the future.

One last thing: Just because you're the boss doesn't mean you're exempt. You need to track your time as well. If you want to price projects properly and you want to turn a profit, then you need to know where every hour goes—including your hours.

148. Every Employee Can Be Replaced

Everyone is expendable except for you and your partners (if you have any). Even the best employee you've ever had can be replaced—and if he or she can't be, then you're doing something wrong. The survival of your company can never rest on the shoulders of any one employee; it gives them free reign to hijack it by demanding bonuses and perks that you can't afford to give or by pulling back on their productivity.

The truth is that, no matter how great any one employee is, no matter how much that person knows and contributes to your organization, if he or she does happen to leave or you do (for whatever reason) decide to fire him or her, your company will survive. It may go through a rough patch, but eventually you will find someone else who can do the job. Everyone can be replaced.

149. Firing Employees Is Difficult and Tricky, and Needs to Be Done Properly

My company has been in business since 1994. Throughout its life, I have had to fire dozens of people for any number of reasons. Each of those experiences had one thing in common: They made me nauseous.

I'm not kidding—I hate to fire people. In the hours before it's going to happen, I wander around the office aimlessly, my stomach in knots, watching the clock and planning what I'm going to say. And even though it's almost never as bad as I think it's going to be—I inevitably imagine angry outbursts or fits of tears from the employee being fired—that doesn't make it any easier.

Still, when an employee is becoming a drag on the company—for example, taking too much time to complete projects or poisoning other employees with his or her a bad attitude—firing him or her has to be done. But it needs to be done right, and you need to take the proper steps to make sure it goes as smoothly as possible:

- Give advanced warning. While you legally have the right to fire an employee at any time due to poor attitude or shoddy workmanship, it's critical that you avoid leaving yourself open to a lawsuit. Disgruntled employees who are blindsided by sudden termination may sue for a number of reasons, including discrimination. To avoid this, avoid firing off the cuff. Document each time the employee does something you are unhappy with—a few typed lines describing each incident should be enough. Then, when the time comes, issue a written warning to the employee and have that employee sign it to show that he or she understands it. Then allow the employee at least two weeks to correct the problems you have found in their performance.

- Although it's traditional to fire people on a Friday afternoon, it's better to do it on a Monday afternoon. That way, they can begin looking for another job the next morning. This will help occupy their mind more quickly and diffuse any anger toward you and your company. Firing people on a Friday afternoon has the opposite effect: You allow them the entire weekend to brood. And while it's rare for an ex-employee to come back to the office with violent intentions, it's always better if you can lessen the impact of that person bad-mouthing your company on his or her social networks.

- If possible, have someone else in the room when you do the firing so that there is a witness who can verify that no threats were made by you and nothing else was done that could trigger a lawsuit. If you have a partner, both of you should do the firing together. If not, have a neutral party like a bookkeeper in the room.

■ Be clear about why you are firing the employee. Make sure he or she understands that it's not for personal reasons. If you like the employee as a person but were unhappy with his or her work, you can fire him or her without breaking his or her spirit simply by explaining that the company is evolving. While you appreciate and thank the employee for his or her work, you feel that you need to move in another direction. Firing people is rough business; if you can do it in a clear way without totally wrecking someone's ego, that's always the best route to take.

■ During the firing, have the terminated employee sign a form stating that he or she understands that the termination is due to performance reasons, not for discriminatory reasons. Refusal to sign the form should result in the employee not receiving his or her final paycheck or severance.

■ No matter how long someone has worked for you, make sure he or she leaves immediately after termination. If the employee has personal stuff on his or her desk that needs to be taken home, make sure that you stand nearby and watch the employee pack his or her stuff. And don't allow the terminated employee to go back on his or her computer; you can forward any personal files later. That way, if the employee feels angry or spiteful, he or she won't be able to steal files or destroy documents before leaving.

There's really nothing fun about firing someone, and if you've got any kind of heart at all, you'll never quite get used to it. But following these steps will at least make firings easier, and will safeguard your company against any negative repercussions. At the very least, when the termination is complete and the fired employee has left the office, you'll have a sense of relief in knowing that it's over and you did the right thing for your company.

150. Lay People Off Before It Becomes Too Costly

Let me illustrate this point by telling you a story. Once upon a time, my agency was flying high. We were doing *very* well. We had about 30 employees, five of whom were earning well over $100,000 per year. Things were going great until one day, quite unexpectedly, we lost our main client—which accounted to close to 65 percent of our revenue. Forecasting a bad downturn in their industry, they had enacted cost-cutting measures, including eliminating certain marketing programs—i.e., us. So that was that: 65 percent of our revenue, gone in the blink of an eye.

Unfortunately, I didn't react quickly enough. Believing that we would rebound, that we would make the money back with new clients, five months later I still had 30 employees, five of whom still had a salary of more than $100,000 per year. New clients were on the horizon, but they didn't come fast enough. Eventually, the strain was too much. The salary expenses had put us in terrible debt. I had no choice: We went from 30 employees to nine in a single day. Needless to say, it was the worst day of my life. Not only was I left with a broken company and broken pride, but I was in massive debt. Not fun at all.

But the thing that really gets me is that it was so...*avoidable*. Had I been more realistic, had I looked at the situation without rose-colored glasses, I could have laid off my expensive employees and reduced my overhead immediately, saving me significant amounts of money and making it far easier to rebound. In the end, we did, of course, rebound—and are wiser and better off because of it. But the road didn't have to be so hard. The lesson? Don't wait until the pain gets too intense to make the hard decision to cut employees. Do it quickly, as soon as you know money will be getting tight, and you'll be better off for it in the long run.

151. Don't Give In to Threats

If employees threaten to leave unless you give them a raise, let them go no matter how valuable they are. By giving in, you'll retain an employee—but you'll put yourself in a vulnerable position. Eventually, probably in the not-too-distant future, that employee will do same thing again. Even worse, when other employees learn what's happened, they'll think of you as a pushover. You'll lose their respect and possibly even foment resentment—not just between them and you, but between them and the employee you paid to stay. None of this is good for morale. As I mentioned in an earlier tip, everybody is replaceable.

152. Don't Pay for Two Worthless Weeks

If someone gives you two weeks' notice, make sure that person actually give you the full two weeks. Usually, after people give notice, they mentally shut down and don't get much work done. Worse, they distract workers around them. If an employee isn't actually going to be doing any real work during his or her final two weeks or it's not totally necessary for that person to train someone else to take, just let that person go home on the day he or she resigns and save yourself the extra two weeks of their salary.

153. Be a Leader!

One of the hardest parts of owning your own company is the pressure associated with it. Employees—not to mention clients and vendors—are always going to expect you to have all the answers. And they're right—the line ends with you. Don't hem and haw and show yourself to be indecisive. Sometimes you'll have to make some tough decisions that your employees may not be happy about—but they'll respect you more for stepping up and being a leader than shying away and being a wimp.

154. Be Friendly But Don't Be Friends

There's a big difference between being *friendly* with your employees and being *friends* with them. Friendly is fine: How are you, how was your weekend, did you catch the Giants game last night? There's nothing at all wrong with friendly, idle office chatter. But that's a lot different than having an employee or two over to the house for a barbecue or going out with the water-cooler gang for a drink during happy hour.

No matter what you may think, and no matter how close you may feel, your employees are your employees. They are not your friends. If they invite you to happy hour after work, it's because they're being polite. They don't really want you there. When you're around, they'll feel just a touch more stifled, unable to be totally themselves. And when the time comes for you to step up, be a leader, and make an unpopular decision—and it will—being friends with your employees will make it that much harder for them to respect you as a boss. It will also make it that much harder for you to reprimand or fire any individual you're too chummy with. So no matter how strong the draw is, hold back. Keep yourself far from crossing the "friend" line.

PART 8

GETTING PERSONAL: MOTIVATION, THE PEOPLE AROUND YOU, AND MAINTAINING YOUR SANITY

When people talk about what it takes to be a successful entrepreneur, they usually mention finances, employees, inventory, etc. The one thing they tend to leave out is that running your own company can drive you insane! It's a career path filled with an equal amount of passion and anxiety, public spotlight and isolation. The personal aspect of running your own gig is every bit as important as balancing the checking account, so take these next few tips seriously

155. Never Do Any Real Work

The word "work" in modern society has a negative connotation. If you think about running your company as work in the negative sense, then don't bother. For you, "work" at building your company has to be fun—regardless of stress. You should think of it as a game, in which you are always seeking the best long- and short-term strategies to win. If it's not fun, you may as well just go work for someone else so you can end your day at 5 p.m. As I like to tell people, if you work a minute a day, you're working a minute longer than I am because I don't consider anything I do to be "work."

156. Ignore People Who Try to Bring You Down

If most of your friends are 9-to-5ers, they're going to give you a lot of flak over how hard. You'll be lectured constantly that you need to work less and enjoy life more. What they don't get is that for you, working is enjoying life, and that in the long run, you're going to have fun of a much bigger variety than they ever will. So I say forget 'em. Don't let the short-term thinkers bring you down. It can be lonely, but you're in this for the long haul. Your rewards might come later in life, but they'll be exponentially greater.

At the same time, being an entrepreneur can be extremely lonely. You may own your own company, but you're still human. You have feelings and emotions that need to be expressed. You're going to need someone who understands you. If you don't have a partner to talk to and don't know anybody else who owns their own company, go online and look for networking organizations for entrepreneurs. There are many of them out there that exist strictly to give business owners a chance to talk with like-minded people. Often, in order to discourage members from selling, these don't even allow business-card exchanges; rather than being geared toward finding new clients, these clubs exist to provide a forum to make entrepreneurs lives a little easier.

157. Bring on the Pessimists

There will be people who don't believe in you. Although you should-n't build your company just to prove them wrong, those people can motivate and push you to work harder.

One summer during college, I worked in a perfume factory, putting caps on bottles as they passed by on a conveyor belt. About a month into the job, I asked to be moved into a higher position. It didn't pay much more—a whopping 25 cents an hour—but at least it would get me off the assembly line. But my boss refused my request, saying I wasn't a "go getter."

His comment never left me. Years later, I stuffed a copy of my first commercially published book, a copy of *Entrepreneur* magazine with me on the cover, my agency's media kit, and a photocopy of one of my paychecks into an envelope, went to the factory, and asked for my old boss. He didn't remember me, but I told him that he once said I wasn't a go-getter and I handed him the envelope. Arrogant? Maybe. But I felt better, and plotting my "revenge" helped motivate me.

158. Believe In Yourself to the Bitter End

Success is rarely a straight line to the top, even if that's the way you imagine it will be when you begin your company. There are a lot of ups and downs along the way. Believe in yourself and in your company, and let that faith push you through—even if others lose their faith in you along the way.

History is filled with people who failed miserably before finally succeeding:

- PT Barnum filed for bankruptcy before finally starting the "Greatest Show on Earth."

- Milton Hershey logged two failed entrepreneurial ventures, losing the financial and moral support of much of his family, before finally launching a business that would turn into the most well-known confection company in history.

- Walt Disney went into personal bankruptcy early in his career after losing his main client but, undeterred, he went on to create some of the most beloved characters in history.

Are you capable of being as successful as the people on this list? Of course you are—although you don't have to reach those heights to consider yourself a success. The point is, believe in yourself. Even failure shouldn't be enough to stop you if you believe in what you are trying to achieve.

159. Seek Out the Source and Use It Often

Find things that motivate you—movies, books, or business people—and go back to them when you need inspiration. It's kind of like finding your own personal coach. But rather than pumping up the team to win a big game, your "coach" makes you want to want to get to work and succeed in a big way!

My own list of things that motivate me include the following:

- The movie *Rudy*. If that final scene doesn't make you want to win, I don't know what will!

- The movie *Wall Street*. Clearly, Oliver Stone's anti-capitalism message was lost on me, because decades later, I still want to be just like Gordon Gekko.

- Anything by Richard Branson, founder of Virgin and one of the most amazing businesspeople in modern history. People get so excited by Donald Trump; in my opinion, Trump can't hold a candle to Branson.

- Led Zeppelin's *Kashmir*, particularly the version recorded during their *No Quarter* tour, with the symphony orchestra behind them. Nothing gets me going like that song!

At some point, every entrepreneur needs a lift. Figure out what lifts you, and put it to work anytime you need a boost.

160. Money Is Not a Good Motivation

If your motivating factors are money and material goods or if you are looking to take more time off and have more vacations, then be prepared for a long, uphill battle with a lot of disappointment. If you are running a legitimate company, it'll probably be a long while before you see any real money from it—and in the meantime, you'll have a lot of expenditures that you probably weren't counting on.

Simply stated, money isn't the primary reason you should open a business and become an entrepreneur. Yes, the potential for a lot of money is there; with great risk comes to possibility of great reward. But that can't be the goal. The motivation needs to come from a longing to produce something—to build something that you can step back from, look at, and feel proud of. You need to be the type that gets restless easily, requires constant movement, and feels greater stress during downtime than during work time. You need to show the world your ideas and your innovations and prove that you can accomplish great things. Your motivation needs to be to satisfy that beast inside you that never sleeps and is always thinking. But most of all, the motivation for starting your own company needs to come from an unquenchable drive to win—to solve problems and come out on top.

Make the right decisions, and eventually the money and the vacations will be there. But those can't be the reason you take the risk. The reason has to be bigger than that.

161. Work the Way That's Best for You

Figure out how you work best and don't be afraid to work that way—even if the logical side of your brain resists. For example, maybe you're not a morning person. If so, don't force yourself to wake up super early; you won't do your best work then. If you work best when you've waited until the last minute to get things done, don't force yourself to complete a project far in advance because it won't come out as well. If you work better in clutter than in a clean, organized office, don't bother tidying up. Working how you're most comfortable is one of the privileges of owning your own company.

Of course, that doesn't mean you roll into work at 1:00 p.m., when the day is half over. Clients start their day at 9:00 a.m. at the latest, so you can't stray too far from that. But as the owner of your company, you have a little leeway in these areas, and can adjust your corporate life to fit how you work best. For example, I tend to do my best work at the last minute. I have no idea why; quite frankly, I wish I wasn't that way—but I am. It's when I get my best ideas and do my best work. Something about the pressure forces my mind to work more creatively, and knowing I have a looming deadline helps me concentrate.

Often, when my company has to make a creative pitch to a new client, we come up with our ideas, and then my employees and I spend the next couple weeks putting together designs, creating handouts, and producing PowerPoint presentations. Everything seems to be all set—except that each and every time, I end up thinking of my best idea while I'm driving to the meeting. Then, to my employees' horror, I present this new idea as an option without having filled them in on it and without benefit of notes, slides, or visuals. And that's usually the idea that wins it for us. I'm sure one day my luck will run out—that I'll wait until the last minute and come up with nothing. But it won't matter; for all the stress and all the hours my company demands from me, working how I work best is one of the benefits I have always allowed myself. You should do the same.

162. Save the Drama: Running a Company Is Real Life, Not a Soap Opera

As a business owner, you're bound to face real, serious problems. The one thing you *don't* need is to make them worse than they actually are. Overdramatizing a situation won't make you a martyr, won't impress anybody else, and won't make you feel any better about the situations you need to deal with. Focus on each problem that comes up, assess it for what it is, ask yourself what you need to do to fix it, and then take the necessary steps. Creating more drama only makes that process more difficult and is a waste of time. If you want to impress people, save the drama; the most impressive thing you can do as an entrepreneur is to build a healthy business.

163. Start Lists—Even If You'll Never Finish Them

Start each day by writing a detailed to-do list of everything you need to get done before the day is over. Odds are you won't actually accomplish it all (unexpected things always come up during the day), but it's still a good practice and helps to keep important things at the top of your mind.

I keep my own lists in an Excel spreadsheet, broken up in very minute detail. Literally everything I need to do, in every aspect of my life (short of eating, breathing, and brushing my teeth), is on this spreadsheet. One list covers everything I need to do for my company, such as calling or e-mailing clients about specific issues, content I need to write for our Web site, etc. Another covers personal responsibilities, including picking up dry cleaning and paying my mortgage by a certain date. Still another list covers everything I need to do for books I'm writing, including content that the publisher is waiting for, interviews I need to give, and marketing efforts to promote the books.

For each list, I try to be as detailed as I possibly can, breaking down larger items into their small components. I format each new list item in bold type and change the color of anything requiring immediate attention (i.e., needing to be completed within a day) to red. Then, as I finish an item, I remove the bold formatting. It may seem silly, but it keeps me organized, and it gives me a small sense of accomplishment to look at the items I've completed by the end of the day. I review my list each morning and update it with new items as they come up. Create your own lists and do your best to keep them current. You won't get through every item immediately, but it will at least help keep everything you need to do on your radar.

164. Go to Work with Specific, Short-Term Goals

Create specific goals, such as "I'm going to make 10 sales calls today." Without specific goals, you'll never know if you've accomplished what you've set out to do. For example, suppose you decide, "I'm going to make a lot of sales calls today." At the end of the day, you've made seven. Is seven a lot? A little? Who knows? Without specific goals based on some sort of numerical benchmark, you'll never have any idea whether you're making real progress.

165. Don't Harp on Any One Issue

Owning a company means having to deal with issues from every direction. Rather than letting any one problem disrupt your entire day, learn to compartmentalize them. If you're upset or angry about one thing that's going on in the company, deal with it, and then temporarily store it in the back of your mind as you deal with other issues. That way, the emotions involved with one issue don't interfere with your decisions about other issues. You can always revisit your original anger later on, when time and circumstances allow. It's not easy to do—it takes a little practice to control your mind this way—but it's necessary if you want to get anything done.

This is especially true when clients are involved. There have been more times than I can count that I've lost my temper because an employee made a really egregious mistake or a vendor failed to meet their responsibilities. Minutes later, however, I'm expected to jump in on a conference call and be pleasant, charming, and focused on the conversation at hand. I can't dwell on negative issues just then, so I put them in a cubbyhole in the back of my mind, force myself to stop thinking about it, and promise myself that I can revisit everything I was angry about later.

When you own a company, problems will always arise. If you can't juggle them in a healthy, productive way, you may find yourself unable to move your company forward.

166. Put It All in Writing

Keep a diary or journal, writing in it once a week or so to vent frustrations or as a stream-of-consciousness release. You'll need some way to express your feelings as you grow your business. Plus, one day, when your company is huge, you can refer back to this record of the early days of intense struggle during your interview with *Fortune* magazine.

Even better, start a blog to chronicle your adventures in entrepreneurship. Use your blog to show the ups and downs of building a company, share insights into your industry, and discuss the methods you're using to grow. Over time, your blog may help get you noticed by potential clients, put you in touch with other entrepreneurs with whom you can collaborate and commiserate, and even attract local media when you have news-worthy information to report; it will also give you an outlet to express yourself, your frustrations, and your success.

167. Take Some Time to Just Sit and Reflect

As you try to juggle friends and family along with an all-consuming business, you'll find that life will move by pretty fast. Every now and then, take some time by yourself—on a quiet lake, in a park, or anywhere else where you won't be found—to sit back and reflect. Think about everything you've done, everything you've accomplished, what you're happy about, what you're not happy about, and what you want to change.

Personally, I try to take a hour or so on the weekend closest to my birthday. Every year, I visit the deck outside the World Financial Center in Manhattan, overlooking the Hudson River with the Statue of Liberty visible in the distance. It's quiet, and I feel very comfortable there. I leave my laptop at home, turn my cell phone off, and look at the water, reflecting on the year. I think about how my company is doing, what went well, what went wrong, and what I could be doing better. I set new goals for myself and try to figure out how I can achieve them. I think about friends, family, relationships, how I deal with these, and what I could be doing better in those areas. Most importantly, I consider whether I am happy and whether my career, which plays such a dominant role in my life, is the right one for me. These sessions help me put things into perspective and give me a rare opportunity to think things through clearly, with more time than I am used to.

168. Romance Can Be a Very Destructive Force

Don't let a romantic interest ruin everything you're working for. If you're still single and on the dating scene, be sure that anyone you date is totally aware of what he or she is taking on by getting involved with you. Make it clear how dedicated you are to growing your company and how much time that takes *before* you dive head-first into a full-blown relationship. But beware: Even people who have been given fair warning might not really get it. Even if they say, "That's fine; I work hard too," keep your guard up. Most people will assume you're just exaggerating or that they can change you, or they'll take your dedication to your career as a rejection of themselves.

Clearly, I'm speaking from experience here. Over the years, I have dated many women. Each time, it goes something like this: We have a great first date. As we get to know each other over dinner, the conversation inevitably turns to the topic to our careers. If I feel like there's a connection, I explain what I do in a fairly understated way. I make it clear that while I make time for relationships, I'm not a 9 to 5 guy, and my schedule can be tight and somewhat erratic. And inevitably, my date responds that that's no problem, she admires my work ethic, she works a lot to, my schedule won't be a problem, blah, blah, blah. Eventually, though—usually within a month—"Your schedule won't be a problem" always changes to "Are you always going to work this much?" And the cycle begins again.

Over the years, I have learned how to create a better balance for myself between work and play and how to dedicate more time to relationships without sacrificing my work. But that only happened after many years, when my company was more firmly established. In the early days, it's more likely that something will go off track a bit: your company or your relationships. It'll be up to you to decide which is more important.

169. For Richer or Poorer...Are You Sure?

Dedication to your business isn't all on your shoulders. Make sure that your significant other also understands that owning a company doesn't mean instant riches. In fact, it's usually the opposite: instant debt. He or she is going to need to suffer along with you through the hard times, when you have to invest *even more* before you can enjoy the long-term results together. Remember: It's far easier for someone to *say* he or she will stick with you and suffer through the hard times than it is to actually *do* it.

170. Determine Your Long-Term Goals

Identify your long-term goals. Do you want to build a small niche for yourself and earn a steady living? Or do you dream of growing your business into a huge company with thousands of employees? While the rewards for the latter are far greater, so are the risks involved. Balance what you really want with what you're realistically capable of—how much work and stress you're willing to endure.

Of course, setting long-term goals isn't enough. Anybody can say they want to own a larger company, but then what? You have to figure out how to get there. To do that, you need to set intermediate benchmarks along the way. For example, suppose your long-term goal is to be a huge multinational company with thousands of employees. Good for you. Vague and lofty, but good. I mean, dare to dream, right? But now is the time to stop being vague and start setting benchmarks. If you're currently a one-man operation, your first major benchmark might be to have enough clients, work, and incoming revenue to carry a staff of five people by this time next year. Now you need "minor" benchmarks to help you reach that major one, such as pulling in five new clients by the end of the next quarter and seven new clients by the end of the quarter after that.

Whatever your goals are, go for them. But be smart about it. Take the right steps to reach them.

171. Quit Complaining and Stop Wasting Time

I once had a friend who was a newly minted lawyer in New York City. Every few nights, she'd call me to complain about how much work she had to do, how unfair it was, how she'd never get it done, blah, blah, blah. One night, after a 45-minute complaint session, it occurred to me that I probably wasn't the first person she'd called. Then I did the math: If I was the fourth person she'd called, and each call was 45 minutes, then she'd complained for three hours—more time than it would have taken her to finish her work! (Needless to say, she didn't appreciate my pointing that out.)

Be a doer, not a complainer. It's easy to spot someone who will fail miserably by how much complaining they do and how little time they spend trying to improve their situation. Movie stars and business moguls didn't get where they are by sitting at home and watching TV or complaining to everyone about how hard their lives were; they made their success happen through perseverance and hard work. Every hour you spend watching TV or playing computer Solitaire is one more hour that you're *not* building your own success. Every minute you spend complaining about how much work you have to do is one minute less that you have to actually do it.

172. Find Alternate Routes to Your Goals

Find ways of doing things even if they seem impossible. There are many ways of achieving everything you want to accomplish. If a road-block pops up on one path, then find another path. Nobody in the world is unreachable, no information is impossible to get, and no project is impossible to complete (although it may not be worthwhile). Be creative, be clever, and don't give up.

Not too long ago, I spent a few months trying to get in touch with a key executive with PepsiCo. I wanted to ask him to co-author a book about social-media marketing for my *Perspectives* series. You can imagine how tough it is to get in touch with a key exec at a global company, especially if you're with a marketing agency! I tried calling; no luck. I tried e-mailing to no avail. I even @ replied him on Twitter. Nothing. Eventually, though, I found my in. I learned that he was scheduled to speak in New York City, near where I live. That was my chance. I went, bringing along a copy of my latest book, *Perspectives on Marketing*, in which I discuss the Pepsi brand as one of the few to which I am loyal. During the event, I raised my hand and asked a question that was sure to be memorable. Afterward, I stood in line to talk with him one-on-one. He recalled the question I asked, and we discussed it. Then I gave him a copy of my book, with my business card marking the page that discussed Pepsi (with the passage highlighted). Long story short, one month and three discussions later, Bonin Bough, Global Director of Social Media Marketing for Pepsi, signed a contract to co-author *Perspectives on Social Media Marketing*, which will be in stores in late 2010.

The point is, no matter how high a hurdle seems and no matter how many people tell you something can't be done, if you want it badly enough and the potential reward is great enough, you'll find a way to make it happen. It may take some time and ingenuity, but there are always ways.

173. Don't Take Advice from Just Anyone

People love to give advice. It makes them feel like they are a part of your business and your success. Basically, it allows them to enjoy all the excitement of owning a company, but with none of the risk. But that doesn't mean you should listen to them. More often than not, people give advice because they like to hear themselves speak, not because they actually have something valuable to share.

That's not to say you shouldn't listen to anybody at all. Listen, learn, and leverage other people's thoughts to improve your own situation. But filter the advice you get, taking into consideration where the advice is coming from. People who have been wildly successful may have some great experiences to share—but their need to boast about their achievements could cause them to overexaggerate and to give advice that doesn't really apply. Someone who has failed miserably in business may also have good advice for you that may help you avoid his or her fate, but that person's bitterness may cause him or her to just try to bring you down.

Once, I spoke with someone who owned a very successful company. He told me some of the things he thought I should invest in and some of the new services I should provide to help streamline production and pull in new clients. It sounded like good advice—and besides, he had been successful with his own company—so I listened. Even though implementing his suggestions would be a considerable financial stretch, it made a lot of sense. A few days later, however, I found out that he had left out one small detail when we spoke: His millionaire father was basically funding the entire business, meaning that he was working with a bottomless wallet. It was easy for him to take on all these extreme expenses; none of it was his money! Our situations weren't similar at all. So in the end, I thanked him, told him I'd consider his advice—and promptly ignored it.

Listen to people when they make sense and when they are looking out for your own interests, but always allow your own instincts and know-how to lead the way.

174. Strike a Balance: Other Factors Contribute to Success

It took me a long time to realize the importance of having a life outside of work. For years, working was literally all I did during my waking hours—and considering I only sleep about five hours a night, that's a lot of time to work! It kept me going, kept me pumped up, and I loved it. But the truth was, I wasn't really making that much progress toward my goals.

Then I read a biography about Chess champion Bobby Fischer called *Bobby Fischer: Profile of a Prodigy*. I had always been impressed with Fischer (until, of course, I learned of his anti-American and anti-Semitic views). My interest was piqued when I read a passage that discussed how Fischer tried to exercise somewhat regularly, believing that staying in shape was just as important for his mind as playing

Chess. It got me to thinking: Here I was, a confirmed workaholic. I was out of shape. I'd lost touch with most of my friends. And even though I barely left the computer, I wasn't anywhere *near* where I wanted to be with my company. Clearly, I was doing something wrong.

They say that the definition of "insanity" is doing the same thing over and over again but expecting different results. So as hard as it was, I forced myself to close the computer now and then. I picked up tennis in the summer and racquetball in the winter. I committed more time to relationships and reconnected with some old friends. I still work far more than people who don't own their own company, but I've pulled back from that ridiculous extreme and found a way to add some non-work-oriented pleasure into my life. And you know what? I've been far more successful with my work successful because of it.

For much of this section—indeed, throughout this book—I've implied (and at times stated outright) that as an entrepreneur, work is all you'll think about and all you'll do. It is. So it might seem strange that I am ending my contribution to this book with a tip that runs counter to all that. But I know that even if you've taken my advice on every other topic, this is one conclusion you'll need to come to on your own. As an entrepreneur, your instinct will be to work. No matter who tells you to slow down, and no matter how many times you hear it, it won't make a bit of difference until you decide to do it for yourself.

So here's wishing you luck in your entrepreneurial endeavors. Enjoy the highs and learn from the lows. Know that when it seems like nobody understands your level of commitment to your work, there are others out who fully and completely get it. And when you're ready to ease up a bit and strike a better balance, I'm confident you'll find success in all areas.

PART 9

TIPS FROM THE FIELD

It probably goes without saying that I could write 1,001 tips on this topic and still feel like I've barely scratched the surface. But in writing this book, I realized that you might find it helpful to read what other respected entrepreneurs had to say on the subject. So I reached out to some people I know and asked them, "What are the most important pieces of advice you would give to entrepreneurs?" This is how each one answered. (Yes, a few of these run counter to my own advice, but if there's one thing that every entrepreneur can agree on, it's that there is no one road map for success.)

Adam Wolf

Founder and Principal Consultant of CellCon Consulting and C.O.O. of Places Everyone

Adam Wolf is the creator, producer, and host of *BizTech Podcast*, a bi-weekly podcast highlighting technology, innovations, and solutions for small businesses. He speaks regularly at seminars and conferences about social networks and blogs as business applications. Adam also teaches a course on podcasting for business in Montclair, NJ. You can learn more about Adam and his companies at www.cellconsulting.com and www.placeseveryone.com.

175. Get a Good Accountant

The IRS can be very scary—and very expensive, if handled incorrectly. A good accountant can assist with properly setting up your new company and catching any irregularities and is invaluable if you are planning to pay yourself or other employees.

176. Get (Free) Advice

You may know your product or service, but do you know marketing? Packaging? Pricing? There are plenty of places to get good help with these areas and more, including the Service Corps of Retired Executives, or SCORE for short (www.score.org); your fellow (or former) co-workers, supervisors, or peers; and your (soon to be) customers!

177. Borrow the Good, Leave the Bad

See what your competitors are doing that's good and emulate that. Also, see what your competitors doing that's NOT good and don't do that! Sounds simple, but it works!

178. Get the Word Out (Personally)

Remember the old shampoo commercial: "You'll tell two friends, and they'll tell two friends, and so on and so on…." Do it! Tell two friends. In fact, tell *all* your friends. You may not know who in your social circle can help you on the business side.

179. Get the Word Out (Professionally)

Join a networking group. There are many out there. Also, use social media—Facebook and Twitter are two of the most popular. Write and distribute press releases. Become an expert. Be heard on the radio (terrestrial, satellite and/or Internet based). But use these tools wisely. You can't just start Twittering "Buy my stuff! Buy my stuff!" There is a right way and a wrong way to do it.

180. Keep Excellent Records

Obviously, you should know where your money is, where it's going, and where it's coming from. But you shouldn't just keep track of money. Keep track of your efforts—your marketing and leads. Continue what works and drop what doesn't. You won't have time to continue efforts that don't work or aren't worth it.

181. Follow Up

Keep your promises to customers, clients, and yourself. If you tell a customer or client that you will have a service or proposal by a certain date, make sure you follow through. It's better to push your original due-date by a day or so then to be late.

182. Use the Proper Tools

You don't want people calling your personal cell phone all the time! Get a new phone number for your business. You don't need a new phone; there are plenty of services like Google Voice that can issue you a new number that will ring wherever you need it to. These services often come with voice mail and other features that you can customize for your business. Also, get a PC or Mac that will serve your business needs—and don't forget to back up all your data, *frequently!*

183. Cross Market

Find opportunities that may not seem like a fit and then be creative. Talk to people who have products or services that might match up with yours. A home inspector might partner with an exterminator to offer a package deal for new home buyers. Be creative!

At Places Everyone, a wedding/party seating planning kit, our primary target market is the bride to be. To expand our business, we've created new products and SKUs that tie into other wedding-related products. For example, we've partnered with local spas and a gift-basket company to create the Bridal Stress Relief Kit, combining our seating planner with bath lotions, spa treatments, and aromatherapy candles. Seek out other products and services that share your target market. You may be able to use their distribution to help grow your own channels.

184. Be Innovative

Look at all opportunities and see how you can fit, even if it's outside the box. At Places Everyone, we partner with companies not generally considered to be "wedding vendors." For example, we work with a local law firm that works with brides to check their vendor contracts. We've done the same with mortgage and real estate companies, which offer other products and services that many newlyweds need. By doing so, we've gotten exposure for little to no cost, and we've been able to reach additional prospects in our target market that we might not have reached otherwise.

Danielle Douglas

President of Inspire Enterprise, Inc.

For approximately 20 years, Danielle sold more than $4 million dollars of one product and almost $2 million dollars of another for *Fortune* 100 companies such as XEROX Corporation and Pfizer Inc. She achieved great success, winning numerous sales awards due to the strategic planning she developed and implemented during her sales career. As an engaging speaker and teacher, Danielle, a certified and credentialed business coach, inspires audiences to be open to new ideas and to take positive action while focusing on the real-world challenges facing leaders, offering how-to strategies, and covering business and organization development. You can learn more about Danielle Douglas and Inspire Enterprise at www.inspiretovision.com.

185. Have a Clear Personal Vision

Every person should have a clear understanding of what he or she wants to be, do, or have in life. Your personal vision should serve as a foundation for your sense of direction. Does starting a business fit into your overall vision for your life? Do you want to pursue your passion and make a livelihood from it? Do you want a more flexible schedule? Do you want to attain a certain quality of life? Have you always wanted to be financially independent, and your business venture affords you the opportunity to make big bucks?

186. Do a Personal Assessment

Not everybody is meant to be an entrepreneur! When considering entrepreneurship as an option, people tend to think of all its great aspects, like being their own boss, living their passion, and earning a good living. What they tend to forget is everything involved in making a business a success, like 60–80 hour work weeks, making less money than we did when we were employed (at least initially), no paid time off, no benefits, and high financial risk. Before jumping into running your own business, perform a personal assessment to determine whether it's really the right move for you.

Here are some questions you should answer before embarking on a new business venture:

- What are you good at?
- What are your skills and hobbies?
- Have you ever worked in a business similar to what you are planning to start?
- Have you ever taken a course or seminar designed to teach you how to start and manage a small business?
- Do you have support for your business from family and friends?
- Do you consider yourself a leader and self-starter?
- Do you have enough confidence in yourself and your abilities to sustain yourself in business, if or when things get tough?
- Are you prepared, if need be, to temporarily lower your standard of living until your business is firmly established?
- Are you willing to commit long hours to making your business work?

- Do you feel comfortable delegating work to others and allowing others to make their own decision?

- Do you have the resilience (physical, mental, and emotional) to consistently build your business in spite of discouragements, delays, or disappointments?

187. Create a Business Plan

There is a saying, "If you're not sure where you are going, you'll probably end up somewhere else." One of the primary purposes of a business plan is to test the viability of your business idea. Are there enough customers who are willing to buy your product or service? It is critically important that you create and implement a business plan strategy regardless of whether you are pursuing financing. A vast majority of nascent and existing business owners do not take the time to create a business plan. Often, lack of business planning is one of the reasons for business failure.

188. Do the Research

Developing a business plan can be a long and tedious process, but it will pay significant dividends if done properly. Business planning allows you to gain an understanding of your customer, competition, and industry. Armed with that knowledge, you can decide how you will promote your product or service, where you will place your product or service, how you will price your product or service, and what people will need to be involved to develop, market, and support your product or service.

189. Know Your Competitive Advantage

A critical component of marketing your product or service is separating yourself from the competition. Why should someone buy your product or service instead of your competitors'? Also, knowing your competitive advantage gives you the opportunity to create value for your customer in a unique way, delivering your competitive advantage to your customers consistently over time. When you flawlessly execute your competitive advantage, your customer will give you repeat business and tell others about you. Remember: The best form of advertising is word of mouth.

190. Know the Critical Success Factors That Enable Your Business to Succeed

Every business owner has critical success factors that are essential to the success and growth of his or her business. When you are just starting your business, marketing and financing are those critical success factors.

Marketing is the vehicle you use to tell your ideal customer about your product or service. The more effective you are in reaching and communicating your competitive advantage to your ideal customer, the greater revenue you generate for your company.

Financing—especially financial forecasting—is critical. Most small businesses fail due to lack of adequate capital. It is very easy to deplete your financial resources before your business begins to generate enough revenue to sustain itself. As part of your business planning, take the time to understand all the costs involved in bringing your product or service to market and maintain your business until you begin generating revenue and profitability.

191. Put Together a Team

An accountant, lawyer, banker, and insurance agent are all important people on your team. Each serves an important role in the success of your business. For instance, an accountant will give you input on the best legal structure for your business for tax purposes and a lawyer can advise you on the best legal structure for your business with regard to liability.

192. Get a Mentor

There are so many pitfalls to starting a business. Often, we don't know what we don't know. A mentor will serve as someone with whom you can share your ideas and concerns and who will be able to provide objective feedback. Your mentor will be an invaluable tool and resource for you. Ideally, your mentor should be someone who currently has a business in the industry in which you want to start your own business. At the very least, he or she should be someone who has been in business for some time and is a successful business owner.

193. Think Like an Entrepreneur, Not a Technician

Most small business owners think that because they are good at their trade—e.g., being a beautician—that they will automatically be successful businesspeople. That is the farthest thing from the truth! It is critically important that you learn the essential skills of operating a business. One day, you may not want to be involved in the day-to-day activities of running your business; rather, you may want to just be involved in strategic business planning. Think with the end in mind!

194. Get Financing

If you are not self-financing your business venture, you must consider all your financial resources. Are you going to borrow money from family and friends? Are you going to go to a bank for financing? Are you considering venture capitalists? If you are considering a bank for financing, it is critically important that you have great credit and some money saved or some form of collateral. No matter what source you decide to tap, you must show when your company will break even and begin to make a profit! Once, when I was teaching a class on entrepreneurialism, one of my students asked a very important question: Is it necessary to do financial projections if you are self-financing your business? The answer is yes! It is extremely important. In my opinion, it is even more important if are using your own capital to know when you are going to begin to make a profit. You have contributed your blood, sweat, tears, and hard-earned money to your project; that means there is a significantly greater risk involved.

Heather O'Sullivan

Community Marketing and Social Media Consultant, Speaker, and Writer

Heather is passionate about inspiring entrepreneurship, teaching others how to become the "CEO of their own lives," and how to increase their personal and professional value by providing value to others. She is a graduate of the University of North Carolina-Wilmington and lives in Apex, North Carolina with her husband and two boys.

195. Decide

There seem to be two types of people who make up the majority of entrepreneurs: analytical types, who never seem to get started because they are stuck in analysis paralysis, and "ready-fire-aim" types, who just pull the trigger and see what happens. Both types can be a problem, but of the two, people who fall into the latter category are the ones we actually tend to call "entrepreneurs." Why? Because the first one usually hasn't *done* anything! You see, an entrepreneur creates something. In other words, entrepreneurs are doers. They may start out as dreamers, but they ultimately *do* something. The first step to becoming an entrepreneur is deciding to do it!

196. Read

A successful mindset is absolutely essential! Educate yourself on the successful mindset and business principles that will be your foundation. There are many resources for this information from authors ranging from Anthony Robbins to Zig Ziglar. *Think and Grow Rich* by Napoleon Hill, *The Go-Giver* by Bob Burg and John David Mann, and *The E-myth* by Michael Gerber are great places start. Decide what you want to build your business on. Do you want to be a "Purple Cow?" Study Seth Godin. Do you want "Raving Fans?" Learn how to get them from Ken Blanchard and Sheldon Bowles.

197. Create a Business Plan

Give creating a business plan your best shot. Follow this format:

- Who will I serve?
- How will I serve them better than anyone else?
- How can I reach as many of them as possible?
- What is the value of what I will offer?
- How much money will I make?

Note that the last question is, well, last. That's important! First and foremost: If your business idea is not something that you are passionate about or is something that you are just doing for the money, please reconsider. In today's marketplace, the consumer is buying from those they know, like, and trust. If you are not sincerely passionate about serving them, they will smell it and run!

One more thing: Don't get too caught up in the details of the business plan any more than you have to (which may be more than you'd like if you need to please a bank for a business loan). They are going to change!

198. Ask People First!

I don't care how much you research, or think that what you offer or sell is wanted or needed, *ask people first*—and I *don't* mean your friends and family! This is the *most* important thing you can do!

We no longer have to rely on the market research of some stuffed shirt or a focus group to know what people want. We have social media! You can't do it overnight, but in 90 days, with the right effort, you can reach people in any demographic, psychographic, or "whatevergraphic" you choose. Let people know what you are working on, and ask them for feedback. People love to give their opinions! But don't ask questions like, "Is this a good idea?" Instead, ask them what their perfect _____ store looks like or _____ service provider does. Ask what they would change about the way they buy _____. Ask these questions in a variety of ways, at a variety of times, and in different places (Twitter, Facebook, your blog, Flickr, YouTube, etc). Not only will you gain invaluable insight (and save yourself tons of money and heartache), you will have begun the process of building your fan club. (Sign up for accounts as you or use existing ones; don't even use that catchy business name you've come up with yet.) This will be a huge head start when your business is "ready for business!"

199. Create Your Message

Based on your own passion and purpose and the feedback that you have received, clearly define what you do. This sounds simple, but often isn't. I hear elevator speeches all the time that are either too vague, like this one:

> "I'm Sally, and I sell ____wellness products."

Please! Don't make me think about it or have to define it or interpret it! And don't make it completely forgettable, either!

Another no-no is making your message too detailed, like this one:

> "I'm Sally, and I make the world a better place by providing people with toxic free cleaning products and skincare, and I'm a massage therapist, and I do therapeutic healing, and...."

Sally may offer 50 different plans, services, and products, but she doesn't need to list them all. She also doesn't want to sound like the other 9 million people on the planet selling non-toxic stuff!

Here is a better version:

> "I'm Sally, and I'm really passionate about toxic-free living. My business provides organic cleaning services and products to help you do that."

Once you have clearly defined your purpose and "what you do," then and only then should you choose a logo, color scheme, etc. All these things participate in "sending your message." The very best way to get the most marketing bang for your buck is clarity and consistency!

200. Your Look Is Your Brand

Your look is your brand, and maintaining it is imperative! If you start with this in mind, it will carry you even farther. You can incorporate your look into your office or storefront and your blog, for example.

201. Your Look Should Make Sense

Your look should make sense. If you are marketing accounting services to a corporate client, the Curlz font not be the best choice. If, however, you are trying to market yourself as an accountant "for real people" and are going for the "not your typical accountant" look, it might be perfect! (Okay, Curlz is *never* a really good choice for business use, but a fun font would work in this case.)

Bonus Tip 1. Be Consistent

Be willing to adapt and tweak, but don't run off with the fairies every time a new idea hits you. Once you have established your brand, you can create marketing campaigns and incorporate some of those fun new ideas—but don't change the brand itself. Consistency is critical! At the same time, don't wait around for perfection, either. If you take the time to follow my first three tips listed, you probably won't do either.

Bonus Tip 2. Build the Lure for the Fish

Start out with a "pilot program" mindset and learn what your community wants (and will pay for). Many people set out to offer what they think people "should want" or what they think people "need." But that doesn't always match up with reality—and it certainly doesn't mean people will pay for it. Start somewhere! Decide who you want to serve and what your ultimate intention is, and then build your product to suit your customer. Next, create your message, including your mission and purpose. Stay true to who you are and be willing to bend to meet the needs of those you serve.

Appendix A

Types of Businesses to Start

There are countless types of businesses you could go into—far more than I could possibly discuss in this book. But figuring out which type of company to start is often the hardest part. I've used this appendix to list a wide variety of potential businesses that make sense for newly minted entrepreneurs. Although any company will require certain knowledge of the industry and/or a specific academic background, the following companies should, for the most part, be relatively simple to start, without requiring you to spend an obscene about of money.

For each of the business ideas provided, I've given you the following:

- A basic rundown of what the business concept is and why people would be willing to pay you to do it
- The market category—that is, whether the business sells to general consumers (B2C) or to other businesses (B2B)
- A brief description of the most viable markets
- The potential for growth in terms of expansion, number of clients, employees, etc. (though not necessarily a measurement of potential income), with + equaling low, ++ equaling moderate, and +++ equaling high
- Whether the business would enable you to work from home
- Whether you can run the business online
- What the potential startup costs will be, with $ equaling low, $$ equaling moderate, and $$$ equaling high

NOTE The potential startup costs include costs for particular resources, such as equipment, required for each specific company type; it does not include costs that all companies require, such as marketing.

All opportunities are listed in alphabetical order. Also, make sure you check my site, jaymiletsky.com, for new business ideas and links to resources that you can use to learn more about them.

Antique, Art, and Memorabilia Auctions and Sales

Market Category: Primarily B2C

Market Description: You'll find sellers from all walks of life, but you'll find buyers among those with more discretionary income, so seek to market your business in places with wealthier individuals.

Potential Growth: ++

Work from Home: Yes.

Online Based: Yes.

Initial Cost: $$–$$$

Anything that's in limited supply has value. Antiques, baseball cards, stamps, comic books, art—there's always someone willing to buy or sell these items (assuming the price is right). That means that there's room for people like you to build a company that generates revenue from facilitating those transactions. As a buyer, you'll seek out items and make deals to purchase them at the lowest possible price. Then you'll turn around and sell them for a higher price to other people. You can really reduce risk if you set yourself up with a buyer first, establish a price, and then find and purchase the product in question at a lower rate. The profit you'll make is your fee for helping complete the transaction.

Baked Goods

Market Category: B2C

Market Description: Anybody who's hungry and likes a tasty treat!

Potential Growth: +++

Work from Home: Yes, initially.

Online Based: You can use the Web as a primary storefront for sales.

Initial Cost: $

There have been countless success stories chronicling individuals who started thriving businesses simply by baking from their very own kitchen. If you're a confectionary wizard, then you too could start a highly profitable baked-goods company selling pies, cakes, cookies, and more to hungry patrons. These days, gourmet cupcakes are especially on the rise as more people concoct new and innovative ways to fit a lot of taste into a small pastry. Selling your goods doesn't have to mean letting strangers into your home, however; look for opportunities to sell your products at street fairs, online, or even to local restaurants to serve their customers for dessert. If you're really ambitious (and have the resources), you can open a small café or retail store.

Bookkeeping

Market Category: B2B

Market Description: Small- to medium-size companies that don't have the resources to keep a full-time bookkeeper on staff.

Potential Growth: ++

Work from Home: Technically yes, although clients who come to visit you will likely feel more comfortable if you have an office.

Online Based: No.

Initial Cost: $

Organizations often outsource their bookkeeping needs to outside firms. The day-to-day drudgery of keeping the books balanced and up to date isn't a chore that most businesses want to deal with themselves, and it typically doesn't involve enough work to compel companies to hire a full-time employee to handle it. If you have the skills and qualifications, this business can be yours. Legally, you'll need to pass certain tests and acquire specific licenses to work as an accountant.

Carpet Cleaning

Market Category: Primarily B2C, though some offices might become customers

Market Description: Most clients will be homeowners rather than renters, and you're more likely to find women being the key decision makers on hiring your services.

Potential Growth: ++

Work from Home: Yes.

Online Based: No.

Initial Cost: $$$ (You'll need professional equipment and a van or truck to transport that equipment from one client to the next.)

Carpets may look nice when they're new, but over time they start to discolor and even smell bad. Eventually, they'll need a full cleaning— but most people don't have the equipment or knowledge it takes to do the job right. That's where you and your company can come in. You'll need some heavy-duty equipment, but there will always be a market for your services, especially in high-traffic households with lots of kids and pets. The downside is that customers probably won't have regular, ongoing need of your services, but the upside is that you can likely charge a good price with a healthy margin for each carpet you clean.

Catering

Market Category: B2C and B2B

Market Description: People who are generally social or who are planning weddings or similar events. Consider marketing to professional wedding planners and local companies in general.

Potential Growth: ++

Work from Home: Yes.

Online Based: No.

Initial Cost: $$

When it comes to catering, most people think of weddings and bar mitzvahs. But that's just the tip of the iceberg. Practically every function involves food, and most party planners have no interest in making the food themselves. Office parties, Super Bowl parties, housewarming parties—everyone wants to be fed, and they want to be fed well. More often than not, the quality of the food will be one of the main reasons people even bother to go to certain events! You'll obviously need some serious cooking skills, as well as the ability to put together a good menu and to present food attractively to get this company off the ground, but once you get started you may be surprised by how many customers you'll land.

Collection Agency

Market Category: B2B

Market Description: Companies that have sold or leased products to consumers or other companies that are refusing to pay them.

Potential Growth: +

Work from Home: Yes.

Online Based: No.

Initial Cost: $

Especially prosperous in recessionary times, collection agencies are the bulldogs that go after deadbeats who don't pay their bills. Sometimes, that simply means calling people on the phone or sending letters to try to convince them to pay up. Other times, it means tracking down property, such as cars, and repossessing it. Companies don't allow non-payments to go on forever; eventually, they hire collection agencies to help them out, usually paying a good percentage of whatever is recovered. If you're not the type to go soft at the first sob story you hear, this could be a good career for you.

Concierge Service

Market Category: B2C

Market Description: Wealthy individuals, primarily men, with busy executive jobs. Look for opportunities in city areas.

Potential Growth: +

Work from Home: Yes.

Online Based: No.

Initial Cost: $

Wealthy people picking up their own dry cleaning? Blasphemy! Clearly, they need someone else to do that for them. Why not you and your personal concierge company? Busy professionals will hire your firm to buy birthday and anniversary gifts, make travel arrangements, secure theater tickets, and any other errand they don't want to do or simply don't have time for. If you're a good multitasker, then this type of company will give you the flexibility to work with multiple customers at once. And because you'll be working with a wealthier class of clients, price won't always be an issue—especially if you're proactive and do a good job.

Consulting

Market Category: B2B

Market Description: Mid- to large-size companies that have discretionary funds and are looking for more aggressive growth.

Potential Growth: +++

Work from Home: Not recommended.

Online Based: No.

Initial Cost: $

Did you ever have bad breath? In most cases, people who have bad breath have no idea until someone they trust politely points it out. That's because people often don't know even the most basic things about themselves; they need someone on the outside to advise them from a different point of view. Businesses are very much the same. Most are so close to their own products and services that they can't properly judge the best direction to take for successful growth. You can make a career out of helping other companies take the best path by guiding them and giving them advice on everything from marketing to operations, service packs, sales strategies, expansion, and more. There's plenty of money to be made being the outside perspective for someone else.

Corporate Video Production

Market Category: B2B

Market Description: Companies of all sizes that are progressive in their marketing strategies and interested in using the Web for greater exposure.

Potential Growth: ++

Work from Home: Yes.

Online Based: No.

Initial Cost: $$$

The growth of YouTube has energized companies to take advantage of video as a primary component of their marketing communication strategies. As videos ranging from how-to videos and corporate overviews to humorous viral video effort make their way online, there's a growing demand for qualified professionals to write, shoot, and edit all types of videos for a multitude of purposes. You'll need some equipment to get started—chances are, you won't get retained by many clients if all you have is a simple handheld consumer video recorder—along with editing software and an understanding of how to use it, but it won't take much more than that to launch a potentially lucrative video-production business.

Custom Clothing/Clothing Label

Market Category: B2C

Market Description: Depends on which market you want to design for. Everyone needs and likes to look good!

Potential Growth: +++

Work from Home: Yes.

Online Based: Yes.

Initial Cost: $–$$

Do you break out your drawing pad after each episode of *Project Runway* and start sketching your own clothing designs? Well, why stop there? You may not have the backing of a big-name label, but that doesn't mean you can't start a label of your own. Pick a market of people to make clothes for, design them, and start sewing! You can work with select clients who want one-of-a-kind clothing made specifically for them or find ways to produce your designs in larger quantities and sell them online or through local, independent clothing stores.

Custom Toys and Dolls

Market Category: B2C

Market Description: Mostly parents of younger children, with higher income levels, who would rather pay more for quality toys and dolls that are customized instead of mass produced.

Potential Growth: +

Work from Home: Yes.

Online Based: Yes.

Initial Cost: $

Can you sew or build things? If so, then you can put together a unique business by creating and selling custom toys and dolls. Many adult gift givers look for more personal gifts than just another PlayStation game for the kids in their lives. In addition to enjoying see a spike in work around the winter holidays, you'll also know that the work you're doing is making a lot of kids really happy—which can be just as important as making a lot of money.

Customer Service

Market Category: B2B

Market Description: Consumer-based companies that sell products en masse and are likely to have customers calling with problems, issues, or questions.

Potential Growth: +++

Work from Home: No.

Online Based: No.

Initial Cost: $$$

Not all companies want to assume the overhead of additional staff and phone lines to handle customer service. Some companies outsource customer-service tasks to third parties that have their own banks of toll-free numbers and own phone systems. Typically, client companies train these third-party entities to understand their products, paying them to deal with disgruntled customers, answer questions, and smooth any ruffled feathers.

Day Trading

Market Category: Neither B2C nor B2B

Market Description: You're it!

Potential Growth: +++

Work from Home: Yes.

Online Based: Yes.

Initial Cost: $–$$$ (Other than your computer, you can basically start with however much money you have.)

This might be one of the few businesses where you don't have any actual clients. If you have some money, have a computer, and understand the various financial markets, you can build an entire company buying and selling stocks, bonds, etc. at a rapid-fire pace, generating a profit between the highs and lows of sell prices throughout the day. Eventually, you can hire other people you trust, give them a certain amount of money, and have them day trade for you as well, paying them a percentage of the profits they generate.

Daycare

Market Category: B2C

Market Description: Middle- to upper-middle–class families in which both parents work or single-parent homes in which the one parent has a full-time job. Demand can be strong in the city and the suburbs.

Potential Growth: ++

Work from Home: Yes (depending on state and local regulations).

Online Based: No.

Initial Cost: $$

If you can deal with a bunch of screaming children day in and day out, then you could own a company that helps a lot of very busy parents. Working parents have a hard time juggling their careers when they don't have anywhere to bring their children, so there is a lot of revenue to be made by providing high-quality day care in a safe and secure environment. You'll have to check your local laws about what types of permits and licenses you'll need. You may or may not be allowed to run a company like this out of your home, but once you get past the bureaucratic hurdles, you can be on your way to a successful company.

DJ (Disc Jockey)

Market Category: B2C

Market Description: Families hosting large events, such as wedding and other functions. Tap into event locations and wedding planners to ensure your company is being recommended.

Potential Growth: ++

Work from Home: Yes.

Online Based: No.

Initial Cost: $$$

Have an ear for good music and a personality that will get people moving on the dance floor? If you can be the life of the party, have a great music collection, and have enough money to buy speakers, lights, and other equipment, you can bring people's events to life with your DJ business—playing tracks, organizing games, and making sure nobody leaves until they've had a great time. Your company will likely find plenty of opportunities hosting weddings, bar mitzvahs, graduation parties, and more.

Employee Training and Team Building

Market Category: B2B

Market Description: Mid- to large-size companies with numerous clients that require training and could potentially benefit from team-building exercises.

Potential Growth: ++
Work from Home: No.
Online Based: No.
Initial Cost: $

This is a great business for individuals who love teaching others but prefer corporate life to an academic one. Especially in mid-size and larger companies, there are many occasions in which employees require training, including for new hires who are unfamiliar with the company, when new products are introduced, when new software or systems are implemented—the list goes on. In addition, many companies invest significant dollars in helping their employees work together better as a team. In either instance, companies often hire third-party professional trainers rather than keep full-time instructors on staff. If you're a quick learner and can bring people together and teach them important information that will benefit them and the company they work for, then an employee-training firm might be perfect for you.

Event Planning

Market Category: B2C and B2B

Market Description: Families and companies looking to throw large events. The typical client will have discretionary money to spend, so look for clients in areas where people and companies are a bit wealthier.

Potential Growth: ++

Work from Home: Yes.

Online Based: No.

Initial Cost: $

People love to party, but they're not always good at the planning and preparation process. With an event-planning company, you'll be responsible for planning, organizing, and managing all sorts of exciting events, including sweet-sixteen parties, weddings, and bar mitzvahs. Plus, you can expand your client base to include companies that need to organize large employee meetings, holiday parties, fundraisers, and more. It takes keen organizational skills to pull off a good event; your event-planning company can take that burden off your clients, leaving them free to enjoy the party!

Financial Planning

Market Category: B2C and B2B

Market Description: Look for wealthy individuals and companies who want to make their money work for them as well as moderate-earning families worried about saving money for their kids' college and their own retirement.

Potential Growth: +++

Work from Home: Yes.

Online Based: No.

Initial Cost: $

People are often at a loss as to how to handle their money. Many people simply don't know where or how to invest their savings to keep their money safe and generating additional income. If you have a financial background, your financial-planning business can help guide people in terms of which stocks and securities to buy, how to diversify their portfolio, and ultimately make them financially better off in the future. Customers will be particularly interested in your advice on saving for their kids' college or putting money away for a new home. With this type of business, you'll see your money grow—assuming your clients' money grows as well!

Gift Baskets

Market Category: B2C and B2B

Market Description: Anybody looking to send gifts will be interested, but look for markets willing to spend extra for premium products. Gift baskets aren't known to be cheap.

Potential Growth: ++

Work from Home: Yes.

Online Based: Yes.

Initial Cost: $$

Although the gift-basket craze reached its zenith in the mid 1990s, these customized packages are still super-popular gifts for which people and companies will pay a premium. Basically, your business will assemble all sorts of products under a specific theme into a neatly arranged basket for people to give as gifts to their friends and family, as well as for companies to give as gifts to their own clients. For example, a "Valentine's Day" theme could include a few different types of candy, some chocolate roses, an "I love you" book, flowers, and more, while a "Get Cooking" basket could include a recipe book, a variety of spices, an oven mitt, and some wooden mixing utensils. The bigger and more imaginative the basket, the more people will be willing to pay. It's a great chance to be creative and build a thriving business.

Graphic and Web Design

Market Category: B2B

Market Description: Companies of all sizes.

Potential Growth: +++

Work from Home: Yes.

Online Based: No.

Initial Cost: $$

You don't have to be a starving artist. Companies of all sizes need Web sites, and there's an ongoing need for quality graphic design whether it's for logos, signage, trade shows, or other uses. You'll need a computer, the appropriate programs (Photoshop, Illustrator, InDesign), programming knowledge (if you want to do Web design), and of course some artistic skill. If you're the artistic type, this can turn into a very lucrative business.

Handyman

Market Category: B2C

Market Description: Primarily home owners, so consider suburban residents rather than city dwellers.

Potential Growth: ++

Work from Home: Yes (in terms of management—most work will be in the field).

Online Based: No.

Initial Cost: $$

Sure, we can all change a light bulb, but for many people, myself included, that's about as far as their home-maintenance skills go. Other tasks, such as unclogging drains, fixing gutters, painting, installing moulding, and changing fuses are way too complex for them to handle on their own. If you know how to do all of these things or if you can find the right people for any job, then consider starting your own handyman business. There are a lot of problems with people's homes—and not a lot of qualified people to solve them.

Headhunter

Market Category: B2B

Market Description: Companies of all sizes that are experiencing rapid growth and looking to increase their employee base.

Potential Growth: +++

Work from Home: No (you'll need to meet with interview prospects; you don't want a parade of strangers in your home).

Online Based: No.

Initial Cost: $

Although I believe in finding my own employees, many companies feel they simply don't have the time to weed through resumes and conduct scores of interviews in the search for the best employees. They'd rather have someone on the outside take care of the heavy lifting for them. As a headhunter, your company can reach out to qualified candidates (even if they are already employed with other companies) and recruit them to work for your clients. It can be a lot of work, but it can also be very financially rewarding.

Housekeeping and Maid Services

Market Category: Primarily B2C, although you may find some B2B clients

Market Description: Anybody with a home, but mostly look for clients without stay-at-home spouses. People living alone or as part of a dual-income family are prime candidates.

Potential Growth: +

Work from Home: Yes (in terms of management—most work will be in the field).

Online Based: No.

Initial Cost: $

If you've been reading all these ideas for businesses, you may notice a common thread: There is a lot of opportunity in building a company based on the chores that other people simply don't want to do. Probably at the very top of that list is housekeeping. Between work, taking care of the kids, and having a social life, people simply don't have the time, motivation, or desire to thoroughly clean their homes. If these are chores you don't mind doing, performing housecleaning and maid services can be a great way to get a business off the ground. Do the work yourself until you build a client list; then begin hiring people to do the jobs for you while you concentrate on sales and management.

IT Management

Market Category: B2B, although you might find some B2C clients with computer problems that would rather pay for someone to come in and fix them than take their computer to a local repair shop.

Market Description: Look for smaller companies that rely on their computers but don't have the resources to keep in-house IT management professionals on staff.

Potential Growth: +++

Work from Home: Yes.

Online Based: Yes (if you're set up correctly, much of your work could be done remotely).

Initial Cost: $

If you're a computer geek, then this could very well be the perfect business for you! I can't think of a company in the world that functions without computers—but not a lot of people really know what to do when trouble strikes. Computers crash, information gets lost, and suddenly companies are in a panic, with no idea what to do. If you get the inner workings of computers, servers, networks, etc., and you're reliable, you could generate some great revenue. Your business will include setups and installations of systems and software as well as emergency problem solving.

Lawn Care and Yard Services

Market Category: B2C

Market Description: Homeowners with houses—not condos or properties where an association is expected to handle all outdoor issues. Particularly consider nicer communities with larger yards.

Potential Growth: ++

Work from Home: Yes (in terms of management—most work will be in the field).

Online Based: No.

Initial Cost: $$$

If you live in the city, then this might not be on your list of great companies to start. But for those who live in the suburbs, you know that every house has a yard, and many homeowners simply don't have the time or talent to take care of their yards themselves. (I grew up in house with a large front yard; my dad regularly created odd zigzags with the lawnmower until my mom finally insisted on hiring a service to take it over. Come to think of it, that was probably my dad's plan all along….) If you don't mind outdoor work and have all of the necessary equipment, you could build a great company by mowing lawns, trimming bushes, raking leaves, and even shoveling snow.

Local Delivery Service

Market Category: B2B

Market Description: Companies of all sizes.

Potential Growth: +

Work from Home: Yes.

Online Based: No.

Initial Cost: $$

When people think of delivery services, they often think of FedEx or UPS. While those options are great for getting packages and materials to recipients overnight and across long distances, there are many times when companies simply need to send an item across town, but without incurring the expense of an overnight service. If you have a truck, van, or bicycle with a large basket, you could provide many of the local delivery services that companies in your area need.

Locksmith

Market Category: Primarily B2C, with some B2B clients

Market Description: Anybody with a car, a home, a door, and/or a lock.

Potential Growth: +

Work from Home: Yes (in terms of management—most work will be in the field).

Online Based: No.

Initial Cost: $$

With a locksmith business, you'll install and change locks for people— although most of your revenue will come from people who have somehow locked themselves out of their cars and homes and need to get back in. I'm happy to say that in nearly 40 years of being alive, I've never done that. Let's hope I don't jinx myself....

Manufacturer's Representative

Market Category: B2B

Market Description: Companies that manufacture products, particularly those that manufacture consumer products, needing representation on the retail level.

Potential Growth: ++

Work from Home: Yes.

Online Based: No.

Initial Cost: $

Are you a smooth talker? Have a silver tongue? Good salespeople are tough to find. Manufacturers with quality product lines are always on the lookout for good people to represent their product lines and sell them to retail outlets and other potential buyers. As a manufacturer's rep, you can work for multiple companies (as long as they don't compete with each other), earning commissions on each product you sell.

Market Research

Market Category: B2B

Market Description: Companies that actively market themselves. Also look to sell your services to marketing agencies that may not have research people on staff.

Potential Growth: +++

Work from Home: Yes.

Online Based: Not completely—some human interaction with the client will be necessary, although much of the work can be done online.

Initial Cost: $

To better sell their products and services, companies need to know their market inside and out—their average age, sex, education level, where they live, income, and other such profile data. They also need to understand their market's personality and mentality—what types of movies they watch, how often they read, where they like to go on vacation, and so on. Further, companies want to know how consumers are interacting with their brand. Are they satisfied with their product? How often do they buy it? Would they recommend it to a friend? Have they seen the brand's latest marketing campaign? And so on. The more information they can gather, the more prepared those companies will be to sell to their market. But because most companies simply don't have the skill set to collect the appropriate data and their marketing agency may not provide those services (or, if they do, their own biases may skew their research findings), they look to outside market-research companies to do this work for them. If you know how to collect and analyze information that would be valuable to companies, then you could turn this into a low-cost and profitable business.

Marketing/Advertising

Market Category: B2B

Market Description: Every company needs marketing. As a new agency, look to start off with smaller clients; larger clients probably won't trust you until you have a real portfolio developed.

Potential Growth: +++

Work from Home: Yes, unless you plan to have clients come to you, in which case it's better to have an office.

Online Based: No.

Initial Cost: $

Every company needs to reach their markets, but not very many know how to do it. Your marketing and advertising services can help other companies develop the strategies they need to create an effective message, find new customers, and jump-start their business.

Mediator

Market Category: B2B

Market Description: Smaller companies who have a gripe with another company but lack the resources to go to court.

Potential Growth: +

Work from Home: No.

Online Based: Possibly (there are online mediation firms that get the job done remotely).

Initial Cost: $–$$$ (Costs will go higher if you want to handle all work online, as a specialized site will be required—and will likely be fairly expensive.)

One of the drawbacks of our legal system is that it can be very expensive to go to court. Legal fees add up quickly and court cases get drawn out in government bureaucracy to the point where it's simply not worth it for one company to sue another, even if they have a solid case and a justifiable reason. That doesn't mean that problems simply go away; companies that have been wronged by other companies, especially in cases where invoices have gone unpaid or services have been rendered unsatisfactorily, still want to settle their differences. To do so, they may look for an outside and unbiased mediator. Your company can provide those services, helping companies come to fair and binding resolutions without having to deal with the costs and time of going to court.

Mobile Meals

Market Category: B2C

Market Description: Depends on the type of mobile meal business. Sandwich trucks will appeal to blue-collar workers; ice-cream trucks will appeal to kids and parents; hot-dogs carts will appeal to city tourists and busy professionals working in city areas.

Potential Growth: +

Work from Home: Yes (in terms of ordering inventory—most work will be in the field).

Online Based: No.

Initial Cost: $$$

With a mobile meal company, you'll cater to all sorts of people who are eating on the run, looking for a quick snack, or simply don't have time to find a nearby restaurant. Serve customers coffee, donuts, and sandwiches by parking your meal truck outside warehouses, factories, and construction sites; sell popsicles and ice cream to kids in your traveling ice cream truck; or sell pretzels, hot dogs, sodas, and more from a sidewalk vending cart. In certain states and cities, you may need permits before selling food. Likewise, you'll likely need permission to bring your mobile service onto some streets and properties. But it could be worth the hassle; in many cases, you'll have a captive audience without much competition—meaning big sales and profits.

Office Cleaning

Market Category: B2B

Market Description: Rather than try to sell to individual businesses, market your company through office-building managers, who may retain you to clean all the offices in a single building.

Potential Growth: ++

Work from Home: Yes (to manage, but most work will be done in the field).

Online Based: No.

Initial Cost: $

This may not be the most glamorous job, but it's one that's always in demand. Your office-cleaning business can provide much-needed services including taking out the trash, vacuuming, and other types of jobs that company presidents or office managers simply don't have time to do (or, more likely, just don't want to do). Better yet, office-cleaning jobs are typically done at night so you don't interfere with the employees—meaning you can keep a day job until your company becomes more established and you are able to hire a staff.

Pet Care

Market Category: B2C

Market Description: People with pets. Especially consider cities, where pet owners don't have the luxury of back yards to allow their dogs to run around.

Potential Growth: +

Work from Home: Yes (though you may not want to, especially if you'll be housing many pets overnight).

Online Based: No.

Initial Cost: $

Pets are wonderful, warm, and loving—but can make day-to-day schedules difficult for working professionals. Dogs especially need extra attention during the workday and need to be taken care of overnight when their owners are on business trips or on vacation. Finding a good service isn't always easy; pets are part of the family, and people want to be absolutely certain they are leaving their animals in the care of people who are trustworthy and responsible. Only a true animal devotee will be able to convince potential customers to leave their pets in their care, whether it's a once-a-day walk and feeding or an extended stay over a weekend or longer. If you love animals, then a pet-care company could be a great way to make money while doing what you enjoy.

Photographer/Videographer

Market Category: Mostly B2C, although you may find some B2B clients

Market Description: Focus (no pun intended) primarily on events such as weddings or bar mitzvahs.

Potential Growth: +

Work from Home: Yes, unless you'll be doing portraits, in which case you'll need a studio.

Online Based: No.

Initial Cost: $$

In all honesty, I wasn't sure if I should add this item to the list. A few years back, it would have been a no-brainer; there was always a strong demand for professional photography and videography services. But as people have become more skilled at using their digital cameras and the price of this equipment has fallen, it's become harder for professional photographers to find new business. In the end, I decided to keep it on the list because, as with any art form, if you're talented enough, you'll be able to find a market for your work. It might be harder to come by, and most of your accounts may come from weddings and similar events, but if you work hard and have a good eye, you should be able to create a good business doing what you love.

Private Detective, Investigation, and Security Specialists

Market Category: B2C or B2B

Market Description: On the B2C side, your market will likely be married people who suspect their spouse may be cheating on them. On the B2B side, look for companies that have a warehouse of inventory or highly sensitive materials that need to be safeguarded.

Potential Growth: ++

Work from Home: No.

Online Based: No.

Initial Cost: $$

On the consumer side, get ready to hunt down wayward husbands and wives and track their every move. On the B2B side, however, get ready to do some real detective work. Companies are often plagued by both blue- and white-collar crime, suffering significant losses through theft of inventory, collusion, embezzlement, or other types of crime. If unchecked, these issues could wipe out profits and potentially run an otherwise strong company out of business. To ward off these threats, large and small businesses hire outside investigation and security companies to safeguard their property.

Public-Relations Representative

Market Category: B2B

Market Description: Companies of all sizes, particularly B2C companies that need a large number of people to see and be familiar with their brand.

Potential Growth: +++

Work from Home: Yes.

Online Based: No.

Initial Cost: $

At its most basic, PR encapsulates the services associated with maintaining the relationship between consumers and companies, particularly by communicating messages through the media. Although PR is part of the marketing umbrella, it really requires some specific skills. If you understand the media, have good writing and speaking skills, are personable, then you may have what it takes to start your own public-relations firm to help client companies forge closer relationships with their markets.

Publishing

Market Category: B2C

Market Description: Depends on the type of books you're writing.

Potential Growth: +++

Work from Home: Yes.

Online Based: Yes.

Initial Cost: $$ (You'll need to hire an editor as well as pay for initial printing.)

Many people dream of writing and publishing a book but often feel dejected by how hard it is to find a publisher. So open your own publishing house! Start with your own book or pamphlet that you write yourself and find a low-cost or on-demand printer to do an initial short run. While you'll be unlikely to get your book on the shelves of major booksellers—at least until your more established—there are plenty of other ways to sell your book, such as at local stores, speaking engagements, and online. You can sign other authors to write books for you to publish when you get a sales distribution channel set up.

Real Estate Appraiser

Market Category: B2C

Market Description: Homeowners, but look to market yourself through realtors and real-estate lawyers.

Potential Growth: +

Work from Home: Yes.

Online Based: No.

Initial Cost: $

Anytime a home is bought or sold or the value of a home must be assessed for insurance purposes or in the event of a divorce, there's a need for an independent party to make an appraisal. As that third party, it is up to you to evaluate legal descriptions of the property, create structural diagrams, and determine a fair market price based on market conditions, location, local tax rates, neighboring homes, and the condition of the property itself.

Secret Shopper

Market Category: B2B

Market Description: Restaurants and retail companies.

Potential Growth: +

Work from Home: Yes.
Online Based: No.
Initial Cost: $

Like to shop? Love to spy on other people? You'll get the best of both with your secret-shopper company! Many consumer-based companies, especially retail stores and restaurants, need to know what the customer experience really is. How is the service? Are the products interesting? Is the store or restaurant clean? What is the overall experience? Unfortunately, managers are often too biased to answer these questions honestly, and surveys or opinions polls can be misleading. So companies interested in maintaining a certain level of quality hire secret-shopper companies to send in pretend customers. These pretend customers order food, purchase products, and ask salespeople lots of questions—without letting on that they are really there to assess the business. Once done, they report their experiences back to the client company.

T-Shirt Design

Market Category: B2C
Market Description: Although everyone likes T-shirts, consider younger markets, particularly college-aged kids.
Potential Growth: +
Work from Home: Yes.
Online Based: Yes.
Initial Cost: $

Believe it or not, T-shirts are big business. The raw material is cheap (blank, white T-shirts can be bought in bulk for an incredibly low rate), printing is inexpensive, and they are always in demand. If you can think of a cool saying or draw up an attractive design, you could easily profit by selling shirts online, at flea markets, or even in stores. I once had a friend who would dip one side of a dead fish (like a bass or something) in paint and then press it against a colored t-shirt, making a super-interesting, one-of-a-kind design on each shirt. She would then go to every street fair she could over the summer, sell the shirts, and make enough money to last her the rest of the year.

Telemarketer

Market Category: B2B

Market Description: Companies that need to reach a large number of people and would benefit from having their products or services thoroughly explained, but don't have the resources to maintain a sales staff large enough to do that kind of work.

Potential Growth: ++

Work from Home: No.

Online Based: No.

Initial Cost: $$$

It has a reputation for being annoying, but telemarketing does work—and even a small percentage of success can be enough to generate a profit. And telemarketing doesn't have to mean selling to magazines to strangers. Some B2B companies use telemarketing services to get their message to key people within other companies that they'd like to sell to. The problem is, most companies simply don't have the manpower or time to make the calls. That's where you come in. Your telemarketing company can do the job for them, reporting back with successes as they happen. The hardest part for you will be developing lists of people to call, although there are services you can use to obtain lists (and very often, your clients may provide their own lists).

Temporary Help Agency

Market Category: B2B

Market Description: Companies of all sizes and in all industries.

Potential Growth: +++

Work from Home: No (you'll need to meet with and interview prospects; you don't want a parade of strangers in your home).

Online Based: No.

Initial Cost: $

Between salaries, taxes, benefits, and other costs, hiring full-time employees is often too expensive for many companies. This is especially true in situations where companies need help but only for a few hours each day or for a limited block of time. When this happens, they turn to temp agencies, which can quickly provide qualified employees who can do a job but work only as much as the client company needs them to. As the owner of a temporary service company, it would be your responsibility to stay in touch with a large herd of qualified people with a variety of talents (design, accounting, etc.), organize their schedules, and mix and match the best temporary people with the companies that need them.

Transcription Services

Market Category: B2B

Market Description: Small companies where the management might not have internal support they need. Lawyers should also be a target.

Potential Growth: +

Work from Home: Yes.

Online Based: No.

Initial Cost: $

Lawyers aren't the only ones who need transcription services. Although the image of the secretary taking dictation has gone from cliché to passé, executives still need to get their thoughts on paper. While some have thrown in the towel and learned to do their own typing, many would prefer to simply speak into a digital recorder and have someone else transcribe their words into a Microsoft Word (or similar) document. There's easily enough demand for these services for an aggressive entrepreneur to build a company from it.

Translation Services

Market Category: B2B

Market Description: Companies of all sizes that service customers from a variety of nationalities and cultures.

Potential Growth: +
Work from Home: Yes.
Online Based: No.
Initial Cost: $

Know another language? Then you may have just the qualifications some companies are looking for. Many companies want to expand their business to reach markets that may speak languages other than English. That means that they need their brochures, Web pages, and other materials translated into the primary language of their desired market.

Tutoring

Market Category: B2C

Market Description: If you want to tutor college kids, go directly to the source, marketing yourself in or around college campuses. If you want to tutor high-school kids, market yourself to their parents, particularly parents who are upper middle class or higher and live in competitive schooling areas.

Potential Growth: ++

Work from Home: No (if students will come to you, you probably don't want them in your home or to know where you live).

Online Based: No.

Initial Cost: $

As the world gets more competitive, it's becoming more important for students at all grade levels to do well in school. That goes for regular classes as well as for standardized tests such as the SAT, GRE, GMAT, and others. Depending on your knowledge base, your tutoring company can specialize in one particular area or offer tutoring across a broad range of subjects. The best part is that there's relatively little overhead; you just need your personal brainpower (and the brainpower of any employees you hire) to show some great results and build a solid company.

Vending

Market Category: B2B (even though end user will be buying the products, you'll need to work with businesses to get the vending machines placed)

Market Description: Depends on what is being sold: coffee, soda, candy, stickers, and gum all have different audiences.

Potential Growth: ++

Work from Home: Yes.

Online Based: No.

Initial Cost: $$

Chances are, you don't realize how many vending machines are all around you. These include the candy and soda machines in many office buildings as well as gum and sticker machines in diners and kiddie rides at local malls. The other thing you might not realize is how many people regularly feed their quarters and even dollars into these machines. Of course, you're not expected to manufacture your own vending machines—there are companies out there that provide the products and the machines that you'll work with. Your job is to secure places to put the machines and then go back regularly to restock them with new products and collect your money. You can start your vending company with just a small number of machines and grow from there.

INDEX

Numbers

401(k), 120
800 numbers, 105

A

accountants, 21-22, 58-59, 152
  accounting companies, 165
  Douglas, Danielle, 157
accounts (banks), 52
accounts receivable, 56-57
advertising companies, 180-181
advice
  decision-making, 16-17
  Douglas, Danielle, 157-158
  listening, 148-149
  managing, 148-149
  O'Sullivan, Heather, 160-161
  Wolf, Adam, 152
antiques companies, 164
applications, 31-32, 34
art companies, 164
assets (loans), 54-58
attitude. *See* motivation
attorneys, 21-22, 59, 157
auction companies, 164
authority (partnerships), 41-42

B

B2B (business to business), 163
B2C (business to consumer), 163

backups (computers), 153
baked-goods companies, 165
balancing work, personal life,
  149-150
banks
  accounts, 52
  credit lines, 54
  loans
    accounts receivable, 56-57
    assets, 54, 57-58
    communication, 71-72
    credit history, 70-71
    documentation, 55-56
    preparation, 55-57
    prioritizing, 72
    problems, 71-72
    records, 55
    salaries, 80
    SBA, 57
    time, 55
behavior (employees), 128-129
benefits (employees), 120-121
BizTech Podcast, 151
blogs (marketing), 93-95
body language (clients), 100-101
bonuses (taxes), 75
bookkeeping companies, 165
bookmarking, 35
borrowing. *See* loans
bottom line. *See* profit

90 DAYS TO SUCCESS SERIES

The first three months on the job are the most important! For those who have already landed the job and are eager to hit the ground running from Day 1, we provide the *90 Days to Success* series. These books provide expert advice and action plans for achievement from executives who have been in your shoes before and want to share their considerable experience.

**90 DAYS TO SUCCESS
AS A MANAGER**
1-59863-865-3 • $19.99 • 232 PGS

**90 DAYS TO SUCCESS
AS A PROJECT MANAGER**
1-59863-869-6 • $19.99 • 376 PGS

**90 DAYS TO SUCCESS
IN FUNDRAISING**
1-59863-876-9 • $19.99 • 272 PGS

**90 DAYS TO SUCCESS
IN CONSULTING**
1-4354-5442-1 • $19.99 • 336 PGS

**90 DAYS TO SUCCESS
IN GRANT WRITING**
1-4354-5486-3 • $19.99 • 272 PGS

101 SERIES

Create the perfect résumé. Ace the interview. Hone your skills. Books in the *101* series provide complete "get the job" advice from career experts for anyone seeking new employment. Tips are presented in an easy-to-read, pithy format, and each book is only $12.99 so getting the new job doesn't have to break the bank!

101 GREAT RÉSUMÉS
THIRD EDITION
1-59863-855-6 • $12.99 • 216 PGS

**101 WAYS TO MAKE YOURSELF
INDISPENSABLE AT WORK**
1-4354-5432-4 • $12.99 • 208 PGS

**101 SMART QUESTIONS
TO ASK ON YOUR INTERVIEW**
THIRD EDITION
1-59863-854-8 • $12.99 • 168 PGS

**101 GREAT ANSWERS
TO THE TOUGHEST
INTERVIEW QUESTIONS**
SIXTH EDITION
1-59863-853-X • $12.99 • 200 PGS

PERSPECTIVES™ SERIES

Ever wonder what your clients, customers, or employees *really* think of the job you're doing? Find out with the *Perspectives*™ series. In *Perspectives*, two or more successful executives share their opinions, but never collaborate, ensuring unbiased and unfiltered views of business topics such as increasing sales, building brands, marketing tactics, and managing employees. The frank "he said/she said" format of these books provides a unique learning experience as well as an entertaining read!

**PERSPECTIVES
ON INCREASING SALES**
1-59863-874-2 • $29.99 • 311 PGS

**PERSPECTIVES
ON BRANDING**
1-59863-872-6 • $29.99 • 276 PGS

**PERSPECTIVES
ON MANAGING EMPLOYEES**
1-59863-873-4 • $29.99 • 300 PGS

**PERSPECTIVES
ON MARKETING**
1-59863-871-8 • $29.99 • 377 PGS